ATHLETES

◆ ◆ ◆

AMERICAN
INDIAN LIVES

ATHLETES

• • •

Nathan Aaseng

Facts On File®

AN INFOBASE HOLDINGS COMPANY

On the cover: (left) Photo of John Meyers (National Baseball Library & Archive, Cooperstown, N.Y.); (right) Photo of Ryneldi Becenti (courtesy of Arizona State University)

Athletes

Copyright © 1995 by Nathan Aaseng

Facts On File, Inc.
460 Park Avenue South
New York NY 10016

Library of Congress Cataloging-in-Publication Data

Aaseng, Nathan.
    Athletes / Nathan Aaseng.
      p. cm.   —   (American Indian lives)
    Includes bibliographical references and index.
    ISBN 0-8160-3019-7
    1. Indian athletes—United States—Biography—Juvenile literature.
    2. Indians of North America—Biography—Juvenile literature.
    [1. Athletes. 2. Indians of North America—Biography.] I. Title.
    II. Series: American Indian lives (New York, N.Y.)
    GV697.A1A197 1995
    796'.092'2—dc20
    [B]   94-12469

Text design by Ellen Levine
Cover design by Nora Wertz

Printed in the United States of America

MP FOF 10 9 8 7 6 5 4 3 2 1

This book is printed on acid-free paper.

CONTENTS

◆ ◆ ◆

To my parents

◆ ◆ ◆

ACKNOWLEDGMENTS

◆ ◆ ◆

I would like to express my appreciation for the assistance of Henry Boucha, Kitty O'Neil, Leatrice Big Crow, the SuAnne Big Crow Memorial Foundation, the Crow Wing County (MN) Historical Society, the Cumberland County (PA) Historical Society, the National Baseball Hall of Fame & Museum, Arizona State University, the University of Washington, the University of Illinois, Nancy Hobbs, Elizabeth Petersen, and especially my editor, Nicole Bowen, for making this project possible.

THE VANISHING INDIAN ATHLETE

◆ ◆ ◆

The World Series had already taken root as an American fall classic when Charlie Bender toed the pitching rubber during game one of the 1911 series. Bender had emerged as the "money" pitcher of the powerhouse Philadelphia A's. Pressure situations such as the World Series were the oxygen that fanned his competitive flame.

Bender and his pitching opponent, Christy Matthewson of the New York Giants, staged a brilliant duel through six innings. As the shadows of the stands crept out over the field in the late afternoon, John Meyers strode to the batter's box to try his luck against Philadelphia's top gun. With the confidence of a man who had pounded National League pitchers for a .332 average during regular season, baseball's best catcher cocked his huge, heavy bat and waited. Bender rocked back and fired a fastball. Meyers swung.

At that moment, Native American prominence in American athletics was soaring to its peak. "Chief" Bender and "Chief" Meyers commanded center stage in the most popular sporting event in the United States. The following summer, Lewis Tewanima challenged the great distance runners of Europe and won the silver medal in the Olympic 10,000-meter run. At those same Olympics, Jim Thorpe stunned the world with one of the most spectacular all-around athletic exhibitions ever. A few months later, Thorpe shredded college football defenses while leading the all-Indian Carlisle team to within one point of an undefeated season.

Little wonder that many sports fans in the United States

Charlie Bender, limbering up in front of the Philadelphia A's' dugout, displays the unswerving concentration that enabled him to shine in postseason action. (National Baseball Library & Archive, Cooperstown, N.Y.)

looked on Native Americans as natural athletes.

But like a meteor streaking across the sky, consumed by its own flames, Native American participation in sports suddenly burned out. With few exceptions, the "natural athletes" quit the playing field. Author John Steckbeck, commenting in 1951, wrote that Indians had "vanished from the American sports scene forever."

Steckbeck exaggerated; Native American athletes continue to excel at sports. Yet they are barely visible. Few of them in recent decades have joined the ranks of the celebrities. For the most part, Native American presence in sports has been reduced to mascots, their customs used as fodder for mimicry by boisterous fans.

Native American Sports Heritage

◆ ◆ ◆

Several advantages helped Native Americans rise to prominence in the infant stages of organized American sports. Early European settlers in the United States tended to look upon sports as a waste of time and energy. The prevailing view of their culture was that those who frittered away their hours playing games did not accomplish anything worthwhile.

This nose-to-the-grindstone outlook cast a blanket of suspicion over sports organizers. The average person lumped sports promoters in the same category as whiskey bootleggers and gamblers. Until early in the 20th century, American sporting events usually attracted a rough, unsavory crowd. Fights and rowdy behavior were so commonplace in these contests that umpires frequently had to defend their decisions with their fists. Proper ladies would never dream of attending, much less participating in, an athletic contest.

In contrast, American Indians treated games not as frivolous leisure activities but as an important element of their culture. Native American societies developed athletic contests that were closely connected to their traditions and way of life. Their games promoted social interaction and were often tied into spiritual and religious ceremonies.

Explorers in the 17th century reported on a Native American team sport involving racquets and a ball. The object of the game was to hurl a ball, often made from hair stuffed into deerskin, across the opponent's goal line. Referees sometimes served as human goal markers; trees and other permanent objects were also used. The Indians used words meaning "ball game," when speaking of the game. French travelers, however, dubbed it *jeu de la crosse* (game of the stick): hence, *lacrosse* became the accepted name.

Lacrosse was truly the great American sport, played by Native Americans everywhere in North America except the Southwest. Indians played for community pride, with one village often challenging another in lively matches.

The Native Americans' pursuit of excellence in their team sports amazed European travelers. One early explorer declared that the Choctaw were "addicted" to a game called *chungke*, in which they tossed spears at a rolling disk.

The team concept was all-important in Indian games; individual achievements in lacrosse went generally unrecognized. An 18th-century Choctaw player named Tulluck-chish-ko (He Who Drinks the Juice of the Stone) proved the rare exception, thoroughly dominating games among his people. But it was a white visitor, not an Indian, who felt the need to immortalize the star athlete by painting his portrait. The concepts of superstars, Most Valuable Players, and Halls of Fame would have been totally foreign to Native Americans.

Native American athletes were most likely to achieve personal recognition in an individual sport such as running, the most universal and popular of all Indian sports. Since running was the primary, and often only, means of transportation among Native Americans, they placed a high value on speed and endurance. This emphasis produced runners whose performances astounded their less aerobically inclined white neighbors.

Few easterners of the 19th century dared to challenge a Seneca Indian at any race longer than a sprint. County fairs in New York banned Indians from many distance races to give non-Indians a chance to compete for medals.

Louis "Deerfoot" Bennett, a Seneca of the Cattaraugus reservation near Buffalo, New York, was the most heralded runner of his time. He traveled to England in 1861 to challenge that country's top professional runners. English curiosity about Indians lent a circuslike atmosphere to the races. Nonetheless, Deerfoot not only won most of his races but set well-documented world records such as one for running 11 miles, 970 yards in one hour and for a 10-mile clocking of 51 minutes, 26 seconds.

The Indian runners of the Plains and Southwest, far removed from the white population centers of the East, were not tested under the tightly controlled conditions required for certification of records. But travelers brought back reports of breathtaking feats of speed and endurance.

The Pawnee of the Great Plains, for example, enjoyed a long-standing reputation as a nation of runners. In 1876 the U.S. Army enlisted several Pawnee scouts to guide its actions against the Sioux and Cheyenne. At the conclusion of the 1876 campaign, these scouts reported to the army barracks at Sydney, Nebraska, to be formally discharged from service.

While the Pawnees were waiting for their release, cavalry officer Luther North decided to test the fastest of them, a man named Koo-tah-we-Coots-oo-lel-r-hoo-La-Shar, or Big Hawk Chief. With the help of civilian Hughey Bean, North measured out a half-mile course over the flat, dusty prairie and coaxed Big Hawk Chief into running a timed mile.

North carefully arranged the trial to ensure accuracy. He and Bean timed Big Hawk Chief with separate stop watches. The Pawnee scout cruised effortlessly over the course in two minutes flat. To North's amazement, Big Hawk Chief maintained that scorching pace during a second half mile. Both North and Bean clocked him in 3:58 over the mile distance. North stared at his watch, refusing to trust what he had just witnessed. According to his written report, "We didn't believe the track was right and had it remeasured with steel tape." This confirmed the course was accurate.

According to the official records, no human broke the fabled four-minute-mile barrier until Great Britain's Roger Bannister managed the feat, to great public fanfare, in 1954. But Luther North's attention to detail and his reputation for honesty built a legitimate basis for the claim that Big Hawk Chief beat Bannister to the mark by 78 years!

Native Americans reserved some sports for males, but women

also took an active part in competitive contests. In a large track meet sponsored by the U.S. Army in 1868, a 17-year-old Apache girl named Isha-kay-nay easily won the half-mile race against a hundred Navajo and Apache runners.

Native Americans could not have so clearly demonstrated their physical talents to non-Indians without access to white society's sports. When organized sports began to flourish at the close of the 19th century, Americans adopted a peculiar split stance toward minority participation. Blacks could not play. White Americans drummed the few African-Americans in pro baseball out of the league. Pro football, basketball, hockey, boxing, and even U.S. Olympic organizations also kept unwritten agreements banning blacks.

At the same time, these organizations accepted Native Americans. A large segment of white society felt guilty about the way the Indians had been treated. Reports of army atrocities and of Native Americans struggling on barren reservations pricked consciences, particularly in the East, where organized sports were centered. Why the plight of Indians stirred whites when the plight of blacks did not remains a mystery. Some historians believe it may have had to do with the whites' romantic view of Indians. Many whites lauded Native Americans as "noble savages" who displayed traits of strength, dignity, and courage that modern industrial society was eroding. Sports teams played into this attitude by adopting Indian nicknames.

Native American athletes also gained entrance to white sports through schools whose goal was to bring Indians into white society. The most famous of these was the Carlisle Indian Industrial School, founded in Cumberland County, Pennsylvania, in 1871.

Carlisle admitted students from their early teens to as old as 23, and its older students competed against colleges in athletics. The school was a well-intentioned but smugly superior attempt to help Native Americans blend into white society. Both attitudes shone through in its motto: "To civilize the Indian, get him into civilization; to keep him civilized, let him stay."

Carlisle used sports as one of its "civilizing" tools. Its recruiters scoured the country for top Native American athletes and found

Led by the legendary Jim Thorpe (helmeted in right foreground), the Carlisle Indians take the field. (Cumberland County Historical Society)

Indians not only willing but eager to compete against whites in sports. According to one Carlisle coach, "On the athletic field, where the struggle was man to man, they felt that the Indian had his first even break, and they were determined to show what they could do." Most of the great Indian athletes of the early 20th century, including Jim Thorpe of Oklahoma, Lewis Tewanima of New Mexico, and Charley Bender of Minnesota, trained at Carlisle.

The Decline of the Native American Athlete

◆ ◆ ◆

The glory days of the Indian athlete fizzled rapidly. By the 1920s only the still-glowing embers of Jim Thorpe's long career kept alive its memory. Native American baseball stars such as Bender and Meyers gave way to obscure journeymen like Ben Tincup and

Moses Yellowhorse. After a mild resurgence in the 1930s and 1940s, Indian ballplayers faded again until their most visible representatives were mascots such as Cleveland's grinning Chief Wahoo and Atlanta's Nockahoma.

Since the 1910s, isolated Native Americans have pierced the ranks of virtually every sport in white society. Charles "Buster" Wilson carried on the Thorpe tradition by finishing fourth in the 1932 Olympic decathlon despite painful injuries. Jesse "Cab" Renick captained the U.S. Olympic basketball team to a gold medal in 1948. Allie Reynolds powered the New York Yankees to five straight pennants in the early 1950s. George Armstrong anchored three consecutive Stanley Cup champions playing hockey for the Toronto Maple Leafs.

Ben Nighthorse Campbell led the U.S. Olympic judo team in the 1964 Olympics—the same Olympics at which distance runner Billy Mills raced to fame. Rod Curl edged golfing legend Jack Nicklaus by one stroke to win the Colonial National Open in 1974. Angelita Rosul made the U.S. Womens' table tennis national team in 1972 at the age of 17.

Several Native Americans have also gained All-American recognition at their traditional game, lacrosse. But such examples of success have proved the exception rather than the rule.

The lack of Native Americans in American sports, particularly in the major team sports, has been especially puzzling given the promise that young Indian athletes have shown. The most common tale in Indian athletics is of the young man or woman who dazzles scouts and recruiters only to drop out of sports long before reaching his or her prime.

John Levi, an Arapahoe from Oklahoma, burst onto the national sports scene in the early 1920s as the second coming of Jim Thorpe. Thorpe called Levi "the greatest athlete I have ever seen." Competing in football for the Haskell Institute, an Indian school in Lawrence, Kansas, Levi's powerful bursts and shifty moves earned him All-American honors in both 1923 and 1924. Levi played basketball during the winter and did double duty in the spring, starring at both baseball and track. While playing a baseball game for Haskell against Drake University, Levi dashed from the field between innings to join the school's track meet in progress against Baker University. He won the shot put, discus, and high jump while dressed in his baseball uniform.

The American League champion New York Yankees eagerly signed Levi to a baseball contract in 1925. Levi gave a sample of his skill when he batted over .300 during his first year in the Yankees' minor league system. But the Yankees and their fans never got to see the finished product. Levi left the club and returned home, never to venture forth on a major league ball diamond again. "I got homesick. I had to come back to my people," Levi explained.

Young Native American athletes today continue to tantalize coaches with marvelous performances only to drop out long before reaching their peak. Teenage Indian runners in New Mexico and Arizona routinely leave their rivals in the dust but walk away from the track when they finish high school.

Obstacles Facing Native American Athletes

◆ ◆ ◆

The immediate decline of Native American athletes after the 1910s can be traced directly to the closing of the Carlisle school. Those in white society who were concerned with helping Indians tended to look down their noses at sports. Carlisle's growing reputation as the ultimate Native American sports factory aggravated their dislike. Carlisle cut back on its sports programs, and then closed down altogether in 1918. Haskell, too, downgraded its athletic program.

These developments blocked Indian access to those sports prized by American society. While white communities began funneling money into youth sports programs, young Indian athletes in underfunded schools were left without instruction or facilities. Few Indian schools of higher learning existed, and few Indians felt comfortable attending colleges that pulled them outside their culture. Contrary to Carlisle's expressed goal, most

Indians preferred to stay with their people in their own culture. So while white and black athletes honed their skills at colleges, Native American athletes were left in the cold.

The occasional gifted Native American athlete who crossed into the white man's sports world often abandoned the attempt in disgust or bewilderment. Even the famous Carlisle Indian stars were offended by the "win at any cost" values taught by their white coaches. They had grown up with traditional Native American values that emphasized sportsmanship and fair play. Indians considered it bad form to bend rules, fight with opponents, or argue with judges and referees. They accepted physical punishment as a natural risk of sports. The idea of retaliating against an opponent for rough play, common among white society, was foreign to them. Carlisle coach Pop Warner marveled at the way his football players refused to fight even when opponents slugged them viciously.

Even those Native Americans who could function under such alien values were often frustrated by the white culture's style of coaching. Model coaches in white society's sports have traditionally been intense, aggressive leaders of unquestioned authority. John McGraw, who managed the New York Giants baseball team at the turn of the century, best expressed this style of leadership. "I order the plays and they obey," McGraw boasted. "If they don't, I fire them."

The tradition of the domineering coach has carried on, unbroken, from McGraw to Vince Lombardi of the Green Bay Packer dynasty in the 1960s, to Indiana University's Bob Knight in the 1990s.

While white and black athletes have responded to or at least accepted such coaching, Native Americans have not. Their cultures place such a high value on respect for the individual that they cannot concede the right of an authoritary figure to virtually enslave his players. Native Americans expect a good leader to *persuade* them to take a particular action. They do not respond well to orders.

Nor are they impressed by coaches' displays of temper. Their culture views such fits as a mark of weakness. Pop Warner found he had to clean up his language in order to keep his Carlisle Indians from quitting the football team. In 1981 a researcher showed Choctaw Indians and non-Indians a picture of an angry football coach chewing out his team on the sidelines. Viewers were asked to react to the photograph. More than 9 out of 10 non-Indians responded favorably and considered the coach's manner appropriate. An equal number of Choctaw responded negatively. They viewed the coach's actions as inexcusable.

The yawning gulf between expectations of Indians and non-Indian athletes toward their coaches makes conflict inevitable. Both Indian athletes and their white coaches often give up in exasperation. One college coach who has recruited Indian athletes says that Native Americans "don't respond to normal motivational coaching. They never develop their potential because they don't want to dedicate themselves to the white man's ways."

The ability of Native American athletes to adapt to white society's values often depends on their degree of contact with whites. Some athletes in this book, such as Sonny Sixkiller and Henry Boucha, have been raised completely outside Indian society. For the most part, the cultural problems they encounter in sports are matters of insensitivity and ignorance toward their heritage.

Others, such as Al Waquie and Ryneldi Becenti, have been raised entirely within Native American culture. They wrestle with the challenge of operating in a totally unfamiliar social setting while maintaining their traditional values.

Still others, Jim Thorpe and Charley Bender as examples, have grown up with a foot in both worlds. Theirs is perhaps the most difficult task as they struggle for solid ground amid the shifting sands of two cultures that are often at odds.

One barrier to U.S. sports participation that confronts all Native American athletes is respect for their heritage. Olympic champion Billy Mills observes, "White culture does not allow an individual to be an individual. You are an Indian first, then an individual."

In the early days of organized sports, whites often expressed this attitude in open racism. Not all white fans shared the romantic

The dominance of Indian athletes such as Seneca distance runner Lewis "Deerfoot" Bennett lies buried in the past. (Courtesy Nicole Bowen)

fascination with Native Americans. They greeted pro baseball's first Native American players with insults, threats, and mimicking of war whoops and tribal chants.

Open racism at sporting events has diminished over the years, but its burning acid bubbles to surface every so often. In the 1990s SuAnne Big Crow and her Pine Ridge High School basketball teammates still heard taunts, insults, and war whoops when they walked into an opposing team's gym. Big Crow, South Dakota's all-time leading scorer among high school girls, dreaded going to college because of the racism she expected to encounter.

Indians have remained easy targets of comic stereotyping. To this day, virtually every Native American athlete ever teamed with non-Indians has been saddled with the nickname "Chief." According to Billy Mills, "saying that to an Indian is like calling a black man 'boy.'"

Sports writers who would not dream of demeaning any other race can hardly restrain themselves from "clever" plays on Indian culture, or what they suppose to be Indian culture. Thus, a profile of Allie Reynolds was entitled "Heap Big Chief." A *Sports Illustrated* article observed that pro football middle linebacker Ed "Wahoo" McDaniel "plays middle linebacker as if it were the last wild charge at the Little Big Horn." Sonny Sixkiller was described in an article as "the most celebrated redskin since Crazy Horse." A Minneapolis newspaper concluded a story on Henry Boucha by saying, "If Henry continues to score goals, his name may become as well-known as Sitting Bull."

Sports promoters have a long history of exploiting Native Americans. As early as 1861, a reporter covering the Deerfoot races in England observed that promoters were "making quite a fool of the poor Indian, dressing him in all manner of queer costumes, and parading him before a gaping multitude."

A few Native Americans have good-naturedly played along with this Hollywood type of promotion and used it to their own advantage. Wahoo McDaniel owed more to his heritage than his talent for his brief fling as a celebrity in New York. A 6-foot, 240-pound Choctaw-Chickasaw Indian from Oklahoma, McDaniel played nine seasons as a hard-hitting but slow-footed linebacker in the American Football League in the 1960s.

Wahoo McDaniel learned the commercial value of his nickname in pro wrestling. In 1961 a wrestling promoter, thinking that a powerfully built Indian might be a good drawing card, found that McDaniel had wrestled at Oklahoma University before concentrating on football. McDaniel joined the pro wrestling tour during the football off-season and showed a dramatic flair in his role as Chief Wahoo.

When a trade brought McDaniel from Denver to the New York Jets in 1964, McDaniel brought that showmanship with him, with an assist from the Jets' management. The first time he appeared at Shea Stadium, he played to the crowd, which serenaded him with chants of "Wahoo! Wahoo!" Throughout the season, when McDaniel made a play on a ball carrier, the Jets' public address announcer would ask the crowd who made the tackle. The crowd would scream "Wahoo!"

Most Native Americans, however, resent being novelty acts for the amusement of the public. After reading repeated cute remarks on his heritage, Sonny Sixkiller complained, "If I'd been a black quarterback, people wouldn't have written that kind of stuff. Or even if I'd been Chinese." Thoughtless treatment by the press and the public has strengthened Native Americans' distrust of the American sports world.

Some of the greatest obstacles barring Native Americans from a prominent role in sports come from within their own ranks.

In the celebrity-conscious United States, young athletes are often motivated by dreams of setting records and achieving impressive statistics. However, like the ancient Greeks, Indians have historically had little use for records or statistics. Big Hawk Chief was not impressed by breaking four minutes in the mile; only whites such as Luther North found such things fascinating. Just as they were reluctant to give land an owner, Native Americans were reluctant to assign numbers to athletics feats. Whatever the merits of this Indian philosophy, it has not provided the same motivation that drives non-Indian athletes.

Native American athletes have also fought against their peers' suspicions of those who stand out or give the appearance of being better than other people. According to Billy Mills, who grew up on the Pine Ridge Reservation in South Dakota, "a serious commitment to athletic training is not socially acceptable." When Mills set a goal of excelling in distance running, he had to steel himself against the influence of his friends. Some criticized him for trying to stand out. Others pressured him to relax his training and spend more time hanging around with them. They saw Mills' refusal to do so as a rejection of Indian culture. High school athletes skilled enough to attract scholarships from non-Indian colleges often feel similar pressure to stay on the reservations, to reject white society.

Thus, while acclaim and community support surround non-Indian athletes every step of the way, Native American athletes swim against a current of active discouragement. Those who succeed, like Mills, are so intensely motivated that they can isolate themselves from their people. Such a lonely effort is hardly attractive. Peer pressure has dampened whatever enthusiasm many young Native Americans may have had for athletic involvement. According to a study by Joseph Oxendine, "the heritage of sport excellence among American Indians was not an important factor for these young people."

The Indian dropout phenomenon in sports is just a small part of the challenge Native American youths face in finding meaningful direction for their lives. Widespread poverty and social problems have sapped young Indians of ambition, confidence, and hope for the future. Len Kinsel, an athletic director in the Navajo schools at Fort Defiance, Arizona, puts the problem simply: "We have so many whose lives go downhill after high school."

Indian Athletes of the Future

◆ ◆ ◆

Imagine the opening ceremonies of the Summer Olympic Games several decades in the future. Marching under their own flag, in ceremonial dress, come the Native Americans. They are competing as a separate team in the grand spectacle that once showcased the talents of the great Jim Thorpe.

Such a scenario has been proposed by a group called Unite Now Indian Olympic Nation (UNION). The idea has sparked controversy among Indians. Jesse Renick, the Choctaw basketball gold medalist, dismisses the organizers as "full of prunes." Others like the idea but point to the tremendous costs that would be involved in training and supporting a separate Native American team.

Whether the plan proves practical or not, the discussion illustrates a renewed interest among American Indians in reclaiming their sports heritage. In order for young Indian athletes to break through the barriers that separate them from this heritage, they need two things: opportunity and direction.

Concerned groups of Native Americans have recently taken an active role in providing athletes with opportunities to excel at sports. Wings of America is a national organization that supports efforts of Indian athletes to qualify for international competition. Native American leaders have also made plans to launch an Indian Olympics, the first of which is scheduled for July 1995 in Bemidji, Minnesota.

American society could clear barriers to Indian athletes by disbanding the stereotyped images that fuel Indian suspicions of white culture. This requires nothing more than treating Native Americans as individuals worthy of respect and not as exotic remnants of noble savages that once roamed the earth.

A major problem in providing direction for Indian athletes is the lack of recognized role models. In a recent survey of high school students, only 4 percent could name an Indian athlete. The absence of role models is especially glaring in the high visibility sports: men's basketball, football, and baseball.

Even avid sports fans have trouble identifying the Indian presence in sports. Few baseball fans are aware that Jack Aker, who set an American League record for saves while pitching for the Kansas City A's in 1966, is descended from the Potawatomi tribe. On the other hand, many knowledgeable hockey fans believe that former Boston Bruin, Johnny Bucyk, is a Native American. Despite his nickname of "Chief," Bucyk has no Indian blood. Cherokee Parks, the outstanding basketball center for Duke University in the mid-1990s also bears the nickname "Chief" despite scant Indian blood in his background.

Again, concerned Native Americans have taken steps to identify and promote athletic role models among their people. The American Indian Athletic Hall of Fame opened at Haskell Indian Junior College in Lawrence, Kansas. Recently, a national pow-wow honored the 10 Native Americans who have participated in the Olympics.

This book is a similar effort to identify and promote Native American athletes. The importance of such an effort shines through in the words of Donnie Bellcourt, a young Chippewa-Cree distance runner. While discussing the obstacles to his goal of competing on an international level, Bellcourt pointed to a role model as the light at the end of his tunnel. "If Billy Mills could get through it back in the 60s, when there weren't any finances—and he did it on his own—if he was tough enough to do that, hopefully, I have the determination to do that, too."

CHARLEY BENDER AND JOHN MEYERS

◆ ◆ ◆

Rough Road to Baseball Fame

The Indian chants and tomahawk chops that swept American sports complexes in the late 1980s were hardly original with that generation. More than 80 years earlier, fans commonly greeted Charley Bender with the same kind of mimicking. Most were opposition hecklers trying to get his goat.

Normally among the quietest, most gracious men in all baseball, the proud Bender could not ignore the insulting behavior. "Foreigners!" he would shout back at the taunting fans. Bender found professional baseball to be a hostile environment. "I wouldn't advise any of the students at Carlisle to become a professional baseball player," he wrote in 1909. "It is a hard road to travel."

Catcher John Meyers, playing at about the same time as Bender, also discovered that while Indians were allowed in pro baseball they were not necessarily welcome. In Meyers's first game in organized ball, he signaled for a fastball from his pitcher. Instead, the pitcher fired a spitball (legal at the time) that hit Meyers in the gut. After the pitcher crossed him up again, Meyers quit signaling pitches and just caught whatever the pitcher threw. In that same game, Meyers's teammates refused to give him a bat to use at the plate. When his manager finally found one for him, Meyers had to dive away from the first pitch—a fastball aimed at his head. Although some of this was typical rookie hazing, Meyers knew there was more to it. "I didn't belong," he later said as he reflected on his career. "I was an Indian."

Tall, regal Charley Bender and powerful John Meyers each fought through the hostile atmosphere to reach the top in major league baseball. These two vastly different individuals from tribes separated by thousands of miles, each lent a touch of class to a rowdy sport that desperately needed an image overhaul.

◆ ◆ ◆

Charles Albert Bender was born in Crow Wing County, Minnesota, on May 5, 1883. His father was a German Canadian who came to Minnesota, found work in a sawmill, and met and married a woman from a neighboring Chippewa band. Charley grew up on the White Earth Reservation near Brainerd, Minnesota, until the age of eight. His parents believed strongly in a good formal education and were willing to send Charley far away to the East to get it. In 1891 he enrolled at a boarding school in Philadelphia operated by the Episcopalian Church.

He returned home at the age of 13 for a couple of months, then ran away from home to enter the Carlisle Indian school. Carlisle's ambitious sports program steered Bender into baseball. Bender graduated from Carlisle in 1902, a few years before the great Jim Thorpe arrived. Bender played summer semipro baseball in Harrisburg, Pennsylvania, but saved little money. During the winter, he worked as an apprentice jeweler and watchmaker.

While at Harrisburg, Bender caught the eye of Philadelphia A's' manager Connie Mack. Bender could play any position on the field. He had a strong arm, was sure-handed in the field, and hit with authority. But at that time, major league teams were a little gun-shy about Native American athletes. Their first encounter with an Indian ballplayer had been a disaster.

John McGraw, who managed against Ty Cobb, Honus Wagner, and Babe Ruth, insisted that Louis Sockalexis was the greatest ballplayer he ever saw. Sockalexis was a Penobscot, born in Old

Town, Maine, in 1871. He first attracted attention playing in a local summer league and went on to fame at Holy Cross College. In his two years at Holy Cross, Sockalexis toyed with opponents. He batted .436 one year, .444 the next, and tossed three no-hit games in the bargain. The Cleveland Spiders of the National League eagerly signed him to a contract in 1897. They thoroughly expected to ride his bat to a pennant.

The allure of the exotic Indian attracted curious fans. At first, even the Cleveland fans teased and mocked Sockalexis with war whoops and chants. But the Indian's effortless talent impressed them, and Sockalexis became one of the team's most popular players.

Sockalexis responded well on the field to all the attention he aroused. But while he pounded the hide off the baseball, he handled the social aspect of his pioneer effort less successfully. When a leg injury in midsummer cut back his playing time, Sockalexis grew more troubled. In August his manager suspended and fined him for unacceptable conduct. Sockalexis played in only 66 games all season, and his strong start faded into a still remarkable .331 average.

Sockalexis continued to disintegrate over the next two seasons. Plagued by alcoholism, he played sparingly, and his average dropped each year. By 1900 this incredible talent was out of the league forever. Some baseball men began to doubt whether Indians, even those with great skill, were reliable enough to succeed in the pros.

Connie Mack, though, decided to take a chance. Had Charlie Bender gone the way of Sockalexis, Native Americans might well have been squeezed out of pro baseball along with blacks. But Bender, although less flashy than Sockalexis, was dignified, disciplined, and stable.

Bender joined the A's in 1903. Inevitably, his teammates tagged him with the nickname "Chief." Bender stoically tolerated the name. But he signed autographs "Charley Bender" until late in his career when he conceded that "Chief" was part of his baseball identity. Manager Mack, a man so formal he wore a suit and tie while managing, usually called him "Albert."

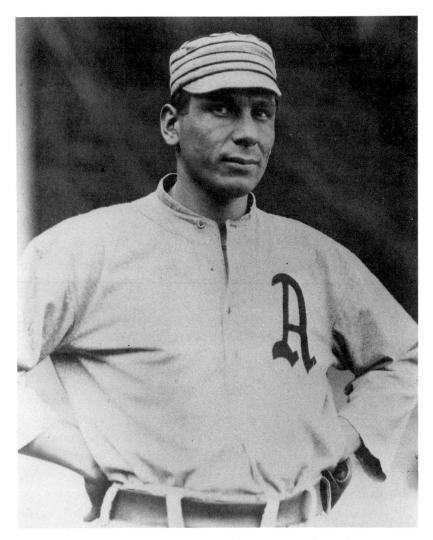

Charles Albert Bender   (National Baseball Library & Archive, Cooperstown, N.Y.)

Bender rewarded Mack's faith by posting a solid 17–14 mark and 3.07 earned run average (ERA) in his rookie season. The tall righthander slipped to a 10–11 mark in 1904, even though he dropped his ERA to 2.87. In 1905, though, Bender took his place as one of the workhorses of the A's touted pitching staff, sporting an 18–11 mark.

Bender, Rube Waddell, and Eddie Plank so handcuffed opposing batters that the A's won the American League pennant despite a lineup that lacked a single .300 hitter. Weak hitting caught up with the A's, however, in the 1905 World Series against the New York Giants. New York's Christy Matthewson had no trouble shutting them out in game one.

Charley Bender was slated to pitch in the second game, and Native Americans took notice. Some Indians back in the Midwest traveled more than a 100 miles just to find a place that would report the scores of games in progress. Bender rewarded them with a masterful performance, a four-hit shutout to even the series.

But Christy Matthewson was hot, and Philadelphia's batters were ice cold. He blanked the A's again in game three, and Joe McGinnity did the same in game four. Charley Bender tried to stem the tide in game five and pitched nearly as well as he had in his first effort. But it was not enough. Matthewson posted a 2–0 win, his third shutout of the series, to clinch the title.

Bender worked hard to improve his control over his scorching fastball and sharp-breaking curve. "Without control you are like a ship without a rudder," he said. "No matter how much power you may have, you are unable to get results." Bender also studied batters carefully, probing for flaws. American League umpire Billy Evans once wrote of Bender, "He takes advantage of every weakness, and once a player shows him a weak spot he is marked for life by the crafty Indian."

Bender's gradual mastery of the art of pitching became clearly evident as, each year, teams found it harder to score against him. Although his won-lost record fluctuated according to the fortunes of the team, his ERA dropped every year from 1903 to 1910.

American League batters did not have a chance against Bender in 1910. The A's' ace tallied a career high of 23 wins against only 5 losses. He allowed just a shade over 1.5 runs per nine innings, and fired a no-hitter against Cleveland. Sparked by Bender and the hitting of Eddie Collins and Frank Baker, the A's returned to the World Series against the Chicago Cubs.

Bender continued to shine in postseason action. He set the

tempo of the series by shackling the Cubs on one hit through the first eight innings of game one. The A's won the game easily. Their confidence boosted, they coasted to the championship, winning four out of five games. The only sour note of the series was game four, which Bender lost, despite a fine performance, when the Cubs pushed across a run in the bottom of the 10th to win 4–3.

Neither his outstanding victory nor the heartbreaking defeat knocked Bender off stride. He was blessed with a remarkable ability to block out the distractions of the past and focus on the task at hand. When his roommate once brooded over a tough loss, Bender would have none of it. "It's a matter of record now," Bender said. "Forget about that game. Win the next one."

That philosophy applied to success as well. "If what you did yesterday still looks big to you, you haven't done much today," Bender said.

Unlike most modern pitchers who specialize as a starter or reliever, Bender did both and also filled in wherever his team needed him. He played in both the outfield and the infield and hit the ball so well that Connie Mack frequently called on him to pinch hit.

In 1911 Bender's ERA rose slightly for the first time in his career, to a still stingy 2.16. Although his relief appearances cut down on his win totals, he managed 17 wins against 5 defeats, leading the American League in winning percentage for the second year in a row. The team, which Connie Mack considered his best ever, headed to the World Series to play an old nemesis, the New York Giants.

The Giants boasted a "Chief" of their own, a man who disliked the nickname even more than Bender. John Tortes Meyers was a Cahuilla Indian born in the San Jacinto mountains of southern California in 1880. After growing up in a Cahuilla village for the first 11 years of his life, John moved with his family to Riverside, California. His skill at sports eased the difficult adjustment to the Riverside public schools. Meyers became especially fond of baseball. After graduating from high school, he scratched out a living as a catcher for semipro teams in southern California, Arizona, and New Mexico.

While playing in a tournament in 1904, Meyers met Ralph Glaze, a former All-American football player for Dartmouth College in Hanover, New Hampshire. Dartmouth, founded in 1769 as an Indian charity school, continued to have a special interest in educating Indians. Inspired by Glaze's description of the school, Meyers applied for admission and was accepted. In September 1905, he set off across the country to New Hampshire, the first Cahuilla ever to enroll in college.

His years of semipro ball had disqualified Meyers from playing sports at Dartmouth. That did not bother him; he was thrilled to get the chance to study. When his freshman year ended, Meyers joined a summer league team in Harrisburg, Pennsylvania. Meyers answered the unmerciful hazing from his veteran teammates and opponents by blasting a home run out of the park in his first at bat. He quickly won a reputation for both skill and toughness.

Before Meyers could return to Dartmouth for his second year, he received news that his mother was seriously ill and wanted him back home. John dutifully returned to California. By the time his mother recovered, Dartmouth's school year was well under way. Meyers did not go back, a decision he regretted for the rest of his life.

Meyers turned to baseball again to support himself. He played briefly for minor league teams in Butte, Montana, and St. Paul, Minnesota. Near the end of the 1908 season, the New York Giants added him to their roster.

With Roger Bresnahan, a future Hall of Famer, handling the catching chores for the team, Meyers could only sit and watch. He did not appear in a single game for the Giants that year. Meyers, approaching 29 years of age, was passing his prime as a player without ever having had a chance to play in the majors.

But the Giants pulled a surprise by trading Bresnahan to St. Louis before the 1909 season. Meyers shared catching duties with George Schlei that year and took over the starting job in 1910.

Meyers's unusual ability to cope with the competitive demands of white society paid off in spades when dealing with his fiery manager, John McGraw. Meyers thrived under the hard-driving leadership of one of baseball's legendary tyrants. "What a great man he was! We respected him in every way," Meyers later said of his manager.

The smooth relationship with McGraw owed much to the fact that Meyers was McGraw's type of player—so dedicated to the game that he would talk baseball all day long with his teammates.

Meyers's glowing tribute to McGraw glossed over the fact that, in his zealous pursuit of victory, McGraw occasionally bent or broke the rules. One of McGraw's ethical lapses triggered a torrent of racial abuse against Meyers beyond the usual Indian heckling. In 1902, McGraw, then managing the Baltimore Orioles, watched Charlie Grant crush the baseball with his quick bat during a Negro League game in Arkansas.

The major leagues had banned black players such as Grant. Moved more by greed than principle, McGraw hatched a scheme to get Grant on his team: He tried to pass off Grant as an Indian. McGraw even assigned Grant a new name, Charlie Tokahama, that he picked at random off a road map.

"Charlie Tokahama" never played a game for McGraw. Charlie Comiskey, owner of the Chicago White Sox, immediately recognized Grant as a star player with the Chicago Columbia Giants. For years after that, fans and coaches kept a watchful eye on any dark-skinned player who entered the league. Charlie Bender, light-skinned with prominent Indian features, was safe from accusations. But many fans believed that the dark-skinned Meyers was McGraw's latest attempt to "put a Negro over on them." Meyers not only had to endure war whoops and his unwelcome nickname, but frequently heard shouts of "nigger!" from the stands.

At 5 feet 11, nearly 200 pounds, Meyers was one of the larger players of his time. Yet, like most players in the "dead ball" era, he rarely hit for power. Instead of swinging from the heels, Meyers sought to make contact. Wielding a huge, heavy bat, he almost always succeeded even against the hardest throwers in the game. Meyers seldom struck out more than two or three times a season.

Meyers batted a respectable .285 in 1910, his first full season as a starter in the majors. As a catcher, he proved he could work well with his pitchers, including stars Christy Matthewson and Rube

John Meyers had to catch some of the hardest throwers in the game with a small glove and little padding. (National Baseball Library & Archive, Cooperstown, N.Y.)

Marquardt. Matthewson and Meyers, both college men at a time when ballplayers tended to be rough, uneducated people, forged a friendship. They were pioneers in making money off their ballplaying fame. Following the 1910 season, they put together a sketch called *Curves* that they performed on stages throughout the East. The act was such a hit that Matthewson and Meyers went on the road with it for 17 weeks.

Meyers pounded out a .332 average in 1911. His top two pitchers enjoyed brilliant seasons—Matthewson led the league in ERA (1.99) and Marquardt won 24 games against only 7 losses. These performances helped the Giants to break a five-year drought and capture the National League pennant. Their

World Series opponent was Charley Bender's Philadelphia team.

Six years after Bender and Christy Matthewson had staged their stylish duel in the 1905 World Series, they were locked in another tense battle of wills. Philadelphia scratched for a run off Matthewson; New York used an error to push across a run to tie. There it stood, 1–1 in the seventh, when John Meyers stepped up to bat.

Meyers knew Bender well. He complimented him as "one of the nicest people you'd ever meet." But he had never before faced him in a major league contest. Bender was throwing some unhittable pitches. New York's leadoff hitter, Josh Devore, marveled, "The Chief makes the baseball look like a pea. Who can hit a pea when it goes by at the speed of light?" When he wasn't throwing heat, Bender was breaking off curve balls that dove for the dirt as soon as the batter started to swing.

Meyers refused to be intimidated. He waited until he saw a pitch he could handle and then drilled it into an outfield gap for a double. Meyers then chugged home on a single to put the Giants ahead. Matthewson continued his mastery over Bender and Philadelphia by holding on for a 2–1 win.

Then the clouds opened up and nearly washed away the fall classic. Day after day the teams looked skyward, pleading for a letup in the deluge. After five solid days of rain, the storm lifted. By then the field was so flooded that the grounds crew spread gasoline and set it ablaze in an effort to dry the grass enough for play to continue.

The long delay gave both ace pitchers enough rest so that they could go at it again for game two. Bender, who must have been feeling jinxed by Matthewson at this point, started off shakily; he allowed two runs in the first inning. But he recovered his poise and shut down the Giants the rest of the way. Meanwhile the A's finally solved Matthewson's pitches and broke through for four runs, enough to earn a 4–2 win.

Philadelphia's renewed batting success led John Meyers and the Giants to suspect that someone was stealing the signs between the pitcher and catcher. Some of that suspicion fell on Bender, who had a reputation as a master decoder of signs. Meyers took the drastic action of refusing to call for pitches; he simply tried to adjust to whatever the pitcher was throwing. The plan did not work. Philadelphia jumped all over the New York pitching. In game six they scored 13 runs for Bender, who hurled his third strong effort of the series. The A's won 13–2 to win their second straight title.

Both Native American stars had performed admirably in the World Series. Charley Bender allowed only 16 hits and 3 runs in 26 innings. Meyers batted .300 over the six games, including his key hit in game one.

With Meyers leading the attack, the Giants repeated as National League champions in 1912. Meyers batted a career-high .358, second in the league only to Heinie Zimmerman of Chicago. His steady play behind the plate also helped pitcher Rube Marquardt set a major league record of 19 straight victories in a season.

Charlie Bender slipped to a 13–8 mark that year. The Boston Red Sox spoiled a return match for baseball's Native American stars in the World Series by beating out the A's for the American League pennant.

The Giants came within a fraction of an inch of winning the title that fall. Meyers did his job, slashing Red Sox pitching for a .357 average. But with Matthewson on the mound and victory only two outs away in the final game, the Giants' muffed a couple of fielding chances that cost them the championship. First, Fred Snodgrass dropped a fly ball. Then, with one out, Matthewson got Tris Speaker to lift a pop-up in foul territory near the first base. Either Matthewson or first baseman Fred Merkle could easily have made the catch. But each waited for the other to grab the ball.

Meyers, hustling all the way down the first base line, finally lunged for it. But immortality eluded him by the narrowest of margins. The ball glanced off the edge of his glove and fell to the ground. Given a second chance, Speaker drove in the tying run, and Boston went on to win.

Bender returned to form in 1913 with a 21–10 mark and a 2.21 ERA. Connie Mack had been so impressed with Bender's steely nerves that he used him more and more as a relief pitcher in close games. Bender won 6 games in relief, saved 13 others, and achieved the rare distinction of winning 20 games *and* leading the league in saves in the same year.

The Philadelphia A's returned to the World Series. There they found John Meyers and the Giants waiting for them again. Neither of the Native American stars stood out as they had in their previous championship duel. Meyers batted only four times without a hit. Bender was never tested and hurled only as well as he had to. With plenty of help from his teammates, Bender cruised to 6–4 and 6–5 victories in his two starts as the A's again triumphed.

Bender and Meyers would never meet again in a crucial game. Now past their primes as athletes, the two began to slide from baseball's pinnacle, although each enjoyed one last hurrah as a player.

In 1914 Bender topped the American League in winning percentage for a third time with a 17–3 mark, including seven shutouts. He performed especially well in front of Philadelphia's fans, posting a 14–1 mark at home. But Bender's career as an Athletic ended in disaster. Facing the weakest lineup he had ever seen in postseason play, Bender was expected to mow down the Boston Braves in the World Series. Instead, the Braves knocked him out of the game and routed the A's, 7–1. The heavily favored A's lost all four games of the series.

Bender's normally unwavering focus may have been shaken by contract dealings. Bender never made much money playing for Connie Mack, a notorious tightwad. Some estimate his top salary at $5,000, others at less than $3,000. Like many of the A's, Bender had begun to listen to other offers. While the A's were winning their pennant in 1914, he negotiated a contract with Baltimore of the new Federal League.

Bender adjusted poorly to his new setting and staggered through a horrible 4–16 year in 1915. When the Federal League folded, he caught on with the Philadelphia Phillies of the National League where he showed flashes of his old brilliance for two seasons.

In 1917 the United States entered World War I, and Bender threw himself into the war effort. He worked so hard in a shipyard during the last years of the war that he nearly gave himself a nervous breakdown. Except for one token inning with the White Sox in 1925, he never pitched in organized baseball again.

Bender coached for a time at the U.S. Naval Academy, then returned to the game he loved as a coach for the Chicago White Sox. In 1939 Connie Mack let bygones be bygones and hired him as a scout and a coach. Bender remained with the A's until he died of cancer on May 22, 1954.

Charley Bender disproved the adage that nice guys finish last. Rube Bressler, who roomed with Bender for a time, described him as "one of the kindest and finest men who ever lived." Yet his gentleness did not keep Bender from slamming the door shut on his rivals. During his final six years with the A's, he won 109 games and lost only 39. He finished his career with 212 victories and a lifetime ERA of 2.46. Those marks were more than enough to earn entry to Baseball's Hall of Fame in 1953.

Connie Mack, who saw plenty of baseball talent in his 50 years as manager of the A's, paid Bender the ultimate tribute. Late in his life he reflected, "If I had all the men I've ever handled, and they were in their prime, and there was one game I wanted to win above all others, Albert would be my man."

John Meyers lost some of his bat speed after 1913 and never again hit .300. When the Giants slumped badly in 1915, Manager McGraw weeded out the old players and started fresh. Meyers, whose average had fallen to .232 in 1915, was a victim of the housecleaning.

Meyers and several of his discarded teammates signed with the Brooklyn Dodgers in 1916. Although Meyers batted only .241, his experience behind the plate had a steadying influence on the Dodgers. He and his fellow castoffs won the pennant that year "by just outsmarting the whole National League," according to Meyers. However, they failed in Meyers's fourth and final attempt to win a World Series.

The 36-year-old Meyers donned the catching pads for one final season before retiring along with Bender in 1917. Meyers attempted to stay in the game as a manager for a semipro team. But during one game, the crowd showered him with boos and catcalls. His many years of playing baseball in the world of the whites had not robbed Meyers of the pride that had been passed to him from his ancestors. With the same unwavering pride as the Cahuilla, who during one brutal winter decided they would starve rather than ask for government help, Meyers left baseball rather than put up with further abuse.

Meyers's pride in his heritage held fast until his death in 1971. In an interview near the end of his life, he quoted an aging Indian leader who compared himself to an old hemlock tree: "My head is still high, but the winds of close to 100 winters have whistled through my branches. . . . My eyes perceive the present, but my roots are inbedded deeply in the grandeur of the past."

JIM THORPE
(WA-THO-HUCK)

◆ ◆ ◆

The World's Greatest Athlete

In the first decade of the 20th century, the Scandinavian countries practically owned the all-around track and field events—the five-event pentathlon and the ten-event decathlon. The Swedes expected the 1912 Olympic Games, held in their capital city of Stockholm, to provide a showcase for the world's most versatile athletes in front of their own fans.

But during two hot weeks in July, an American Indian ruined the party. Jim Thorpe not only defeated his favored and far more experienced competition, he utterly demolished them! Incredibly, he did so without any apparent strain. It was as though Thorpe had casually strolled past armed guards into a bank, cleaned out the vault, and gone on his way while the crowd stood gawking.

The Swedes, gracious hosts throughout the games, did not begrudge the success of the champion from across the ocean. They marveled as Thorpe broke through the known limits of human power and grace to a level almost beyond imagination. Sweden's King Gustav V was moved to the verge of tears as he presented the awards to Thorpe. "Sir, you are the greatest athlete in the world," he said.

Uncomfortable with formality, dazzled by European royalty,

Jim Thorpe during the 1907–08 school year. (Cumberland County Historical Society)

Thorpe shyly responded, "Thanks, King." He regarded this as the greatest moment of his life.

Unfortunately, the golden moment quickly turned to clay. First, came the snickering backdoor rumors. The lie spread that an arrogant Jim Thorpe had snubbed King Gustav and had gone out drinking instead of attending the victory ceremony.

Thorpe easily shrugged off the pinprick of spite. But six months later, his pride was cut to the bone by the stuffed shirt aristocrats who ruled the Olympics. They stripped Thorpe of the king's presents, the Olympic records, and the gold medal victories.

Jim Thorpe soared so far above his rivals that he attracted intense publicity. Over the years, both his athletic performances and his human flaws have been greatly exaggerated. Reporter Damon Runyon insisted that more lies have been told about Jim Thorpe than about any other athlete.

The truth is that Jim Thorpe was far and away the greatest athlete of his time. While comparing athletes of different eras can never be more than speculation, Thorpe has won considerable support as the greatest athlete of all time. In modern times, Bo Jackson and Deion Sanders have won media hype for playing both pro baseball and pro football. But not only did Thorpe excel at more than a dozen sports, he dominated several of them as thoroughly as if he were competing against children.

Equally true is Thorpe's standing as one of the more tragic figures in sports history. Caught in the midst of a clash of cultures, the generous, easygoing Thorpe suffered punishments for reasons he did not fully understand. Devastating personal losses, aggravated by the callous judgment of sports officials, stripped away Thorpe's strengths and exposed his weaknesses. The world's greatest athlete wandered through the final years of his life unemployed, sick, and heartbroken.

◆ ◆ ◆

James Francis and his twin brother Charles were born to Hiram and Charlotte Thorpe at their home along the North Canadian River near Prague, Oklahoma. The date of their arrival was never recorded and is open to debate. Jim Thorpe listed his birthdate as May 28, 1888. Various biographers have suggested 1887 and 1886 as alternative dates.

Hiram Thorpe, the son of an Irish blacksmith and an Indian mother, grew up among the Sauk and Fox people on their land in Kansas. His bloodlines reached back to the famous Sauk and Fox leader Black Hawk. Hiram Thorpe created a vast blended family by marrying five wives and fathering 19 children. One of these wives was Jim's mother, Charlotte Vieux, of Potawatomi and French ancestry. The loosely structured family situation created an unstable home environment. Jim lived in several households during the first six years of his life and was barely acquainted with some of his brothers and sisters.

But he and Charlie were close. They shared a love of the outdoors with their father, who was the dominant influence in their lives. Hiram Thorpe, a farmer, stood over 6 feet tall and weighed 225 pounds. According to his son, he was "the undisputed champion in sprinting, wrestling, swimming, high jumping, broad jumping, and horseback riding." He loved to take his sons hunting, but he refused to coddle them. Hiram expected the boys to keep up with him as he ran across the hills, through the woods, and across streams in search of game, covering as many as 30 miles in a day. The boys didn't mind; this was simply another form of their favorite game—follow the leader. When their dad was not around, Jim and Charlie thrived on the freedom of roaming unrestricted through those same lands.

Jim grew up in a blended culture as well as a blended family. His parents raised him among Indians, observed many Indian customs, and gave him the Indian name of Wa-Tho-Huck, which means "Bright Path." At the same time, they adopted the clothing style and other ways of the whites.

Hiram Thorpe had learned the value of the white people's system of education while attending a Methodist school in Kansas. He was determined that his children would undergo similiar instruction. The thought of spending their days cooped up in a room dismayed Jim and Charlie. When they were six or seven, Hiram had to all but drag them to the Sauk and Fox Indian Agency school about 20 miles from home.

Jim hated the school with its rigid schedule and rules. Ringing bells ruled every moment of his life, telling him when to get up, eat, attend classes, work, and go to bed. The teachers were poorly educated and had little patience with Indian children. As part of the "civilizing process," the school ignored Indian names and banned the children from playing traditional Indian games.

Jim rebelled against the restrictions. Unlike Charlie, whom teachers described as "nice and gentle," Jim took on the role of class clown. At least one teacher considered him "incorrigible."

Occasionally, Jim would head into the woods for a day or run away back to his home.

Jim's high-spirited defiance took on a bitter edge at the age of eight when Charlie died of pneumonia. Robbed of his closest companion, Jim fell into long periods of silence and isolation. He would disappear from school with a dog and his hunting rifle for days. Once Jim's dad brought him to school in a wagon and then turned for home. Jim broke loose from his "captors," took a short cut, and greeted a startled Hiram Thorpe, who had returned with the wagon.

Hiram finally had enough. In 1898 he sent his 10-year-old boy far away to the Haskell Institute in Lawrence, Kansas. The military-style discipline at Haskell clamped down on the free-spirited Indian even more harshly than Jim's previous school. But now, 300 miles from home and in unfamiliar country, he had no choice but to adapt.

At Haskell, Thorpe watched the older boys compete at a white man's game called football. Fascinated by the rough contact sport, he organized football games among his friends.

Jim lasted three years at the school before he returned home, unscheduled as usual. His restless irresponsibility finally taxed his father to the limit. When his dad thrashed him for the first time in his life, Jim set off on his own. At the age of 13, he traveled to Texas, where he supported himself working on cattle ranches.

After proving he could make it on his own, Jim returned home, made a half-hearted effort to attend a local school, played on local sports teams, and infuriated his father with his lack of discipline. Hiram finally took pen in hand and poured out his problem to the United States Indian agent in charge of the Oklahoma Territory. "He is 14 years of age and I cannot do anything with him," wrote Hiram Thorpe, "and he is getting worse every day, and I want him to go and make something of himself and I cannot do it here."

The agent helped arrange for Jim to enroll at the Carlisle Indian Industrial School in Pennsylvania. By this time, Carlisle had already earned a reputation for sports excellence. Jim's placement at Carlisle may have been aided by Carlisle coach Pop Warner. Warner often traveled to Indian territory to recruit student-athletes and likely was aware of Jim's reputation as a baseball player.

In the winter of 1905, Hiram Thorpe sent his son off to school for the last time. He died shortly after Jim left, still wondering if his son would ever settle down and make something of himself. Some of his last words to Jim were, "Son, I want you to show other races what an Indian can do."

At first, Jim showed no more enthusiasm for Carlisle than he had for any other school. As part of the "civilizing" process, the school sent students on an "outing program." This required students to live and work with a white family, usually on a farm. Unfortunately, Jim's first family assigned him to housecleaning tasks. Jim, who probably would have done well at any heavy outdoor labor, could not stand to be cooped up in a house, cooking and dusting furniture. Reverting to his old habits, he walked from the farm back to the Carlisle campus. Jim went on four other "outings" in the next three years, none of which went smoothly.

Although he played many intramural sports, Thorpe did not take part in any varsity sport during his first four years. A skinny five-foot, five-inch boy when he enrolled at Carlisle, Thorpe did not look like he belonged on the same field as the school's nationally known athletes. Even as he approached his 19th birthday in 1907, Thorpe stood only five feet, nine inches and weighed less than 145 pounds.

That spring Thorpe was walking with a group of students when they happened to see the track team's high jumpers working out. After clearing the bar at lower heights, the jumpers raised the bar to five feet, nine inches. Time after time, the athletes hurled themselves up at the bar, only to send it clattering to the ground each time.

Thorpe had been a strong leaper for as long as he could remember. Although dressed in overalls, he asked the trackmen if he could take a turn. They agreed to give him a chance, probably welcoming the comic relief to their frustration.

Without bothering to warm up, Thorpe took a short run at the bar and sprang into the air. As the trackmen gaped in disbelief, Thorpe sailed over the bar without touching it.

Pop Warner, who coached track as well as football at Carlisle, witnessed the jump. When he told Thorpe that he had just set a school record, Thorpe shrugged and said he could have jumped higher if he were wearing track clothes. Warner immediately persuaded Thorpe to join the track team for the final two meets of the season. He also put Thorpe on his "protected" list. That meant Thorpe was withdrawn from the outing program so that he could stay on campus to train.

The next fall, Thorpe showed up at football practice. Warner nearly had a heart attack. "You're my most valuable trackman and I don't want you getting hurt playing football," Warner told him. But Thorpe insisted on playing.

Warner let him run with the ball in his first practice, hoping that a few hard knocks would discourage him. Instead, Thorpe ran through and over all tacklers all the way to the end zone. Warner instantly saw that he had a football star as well as a track star on his hands.

The raw recruit had much to learn before he could contribute to this gridiron machine. He spent most of the 1907 season on the bench, watching and learning as the Carlisle Indians rolled to a 10–1 mark. On the few occasions when he got into a game, he played superbly. "I never had to do much coaching with Jim," Warner later said. "Like all Indians, his powers of observation were remarkably keen."

Thorpe enjoyed traveling with the team. The points that he won as a track man and the praise he earned for his football efforts gave him his first taste of acceptance and recognition from outside his family. Suddenly the ambitionless, rebellious young man stopped daydreaming about roaming the woods and resenting his lot in life. He began to put forth effort into both his sports and his studies. Also, at about this time, he met Iva Miller, the daughter of one of his teachers, whom he would marry in 1913.

Once Thorpe turned on to varsity sports, there was no stopping him. He joined with teammates Louis Tewanima and Gus Welch to give Carlisle a triple threat in track and field. With Tewanima running the distance races, Welch competing in sprints, and Thorpe mastering the field events as well as sprints and hurdles,

Carlisle often beat teams with 10 times their numbers in uniform. Thorpe raised eyebrows on the East Coast by entering eight events in a meet against Harvard University and winning all of them.

In between track meets, Thorpe played baseball. He not only made the school's starting lineup as an outfielder but also pitched a no-hitter. During his years at Carlisle, Thorpe won varsity letters in boxing, wrestling, basketball, swimming, lacrosse, and hockey as well as track, football, and baseball!

But football was king at Carlisle. The team played the most grueling schedule of any team in the country. Yet despite playing every game on the road, traveling from the East Coast to the western plains, Carlisle seldom lost. Thorpe quickly became the star of the famous Carlisle Indians. A late bloomer, he grew to nearly 6 feet tall and weighed about 175 pounds when he reported for practice in the fall of 1908. That was average size or better for a college player of his era, and Thorpe used it to good advantage. He relished the rough play, the high-speed collisions, and the hard tackling as much as the open-field dashes to daylight.

Thorpe's flesh, bone, and nerves seemed to have been replaced with some indestructable space-age material. Although players wore little padding compared with today's players, Thorpe shrugged off the most crushing blows without slowing down. The *Pittsburgh Dispatch* reported that Thorpe "appeared to be impervious to injury." At a time when teams played football so brutally that 33 college players died during the 1909 season, Thorpe hurled himself at opponents with no more concern for his health than if he were diving into pillows. Perplexed by the public outcry to outlaw this "man-killing" game, Thorpe once wondered out loud, "How can anyone get hurt playing football?"

While Carlisle played well as a team, the experts did not think highly of their individual players. Thorpe, the star of the team rated no better than third team All-American. Yet the Carlisle Indians romped to their usual sparkling record against top competition, posting a 10–2–1 mark.

Thorpe left school in the summer of 1909 and traveled with fellow students Jesse Youngdeer and Joe Libby to North Carolina. There they made the fateful decision to play in the Eastern

Carolina Baseball League. In doing so, they followed the example of many college baseball players who joined semiprofessional summer leagues. Some historians believe that Coach Warner may have sent Thorpe and his friends to the summer league to gain experience and develop their skills.

The summer leagues commonly paid players two or three dollars per game. Although far from a living wage, technically, that made them professional athletes who were then ineligible for college play. Eligibility rules were rarely enforced, but most college athletes played under false names just to be safe.

Jim Thorpe did not. His reasons for using his own name remain unclear. Perhaps his sense of honor prevented him from hiding behind a lie. Maybe he thought he would never be found out. He may have had no intention of returning to college and so was unconcerned about his amateur status. Possibly he could not imagine that playing for a few bucks in baseball could affect his status in other sports. Whatever the reason, Thorpe's openness would cost him dearly.

Thorpe's summer league coaches, impressed by his slingshot arm, used him primarily as a pitcher. Thorpe also played some outfield, but he did not hit particularly well. Ironically, the sport that was to cause him so much grief was one at which he had the least success.

But instead of returning to Carlisle to build on his triumphs, Thorpe gave in to the urge to walk away from it all, just as he had so often during his early school days. He played two summers in North Carolina, spending his winters back in Oklahoma.

In 1911 Coach Warner and some of Jim's teammates persuaded Thorpe to return to Carlisle. That fall Thorpe totally dominated college football, with his foot as well as his ball-carrying. The rules at that time placed greater emphasis on the kicking game. Fans often regard punting and placekicking as minor skills in today's celebrity-studded sports world. But Thorpe's thunder-footed blasts gave his team an offensive weapon such as has never been seen in football since.

Kicking long field goals, booming punts, and slashing through opposing defenses on punishing runs, Thorpe led Carlisle to its best season ever. The road warriors from Carlisle demolished highly rated foes such as Brown University, Pennsylvania, and Pittsburgh. Thorpe single-handedly beat favored Harvard, kicking four field goals and rushing for a touchdown. Only a heartbreaking 12–11 loss to Syracuse kept Carlisle from going undefeated. Jim Thorpe easily won first team All-American honors.

With the praise of national sports writers still ringing in his ears, Thorpe joined Tewanima and Welch in preparing for the 1912 Olympics. Lured by Coach Warner's tales of gold medals to be won in the Stockholm games, Thorpe trained seriously at track and field for the first and only time in his life. Workouts began in February. Coach Warner was not the expert in track and field that he was in football. Nonetheless, he knew how to help his athletes get in top condition. The coach made special arrangements for his stars to compete in indoor meets in Boston, New Jersey, and Washington, D.C.

The U.S. Olympic team did not hold tryouts in those days. Track and field athletes qualified on the basis of their performances in the months prior to the Olympics. Thorpe easily made the team in four events: high jump, long jump (then known as the broad jump), the five-event pentathlon, and the ten-event decathlon.

Throughout Thorpe's career, some sportswriters and coaches typecast him as a "lazy Indian." They misunderstood Thorpe's disinterest in records, a product of his Indian background. Thorpe's purpose in competing was simply to win. He often dominated his events so thoroughly that he seldom needed to go full bore. Even when going all out, he performed with such silky grace that he hardly seemed to be trying. As one reporter wrote, "He makes no special preparations for his efforts, and simply meanders carelessly up to his tasks and does them . . ."

Reports from the ship that carried the Olympic team to Stockholm fueled the public view of Thorpe as lazy. Reporter Grantland Rice and distance runner Johnny Hayes spread the story that Thorpe did not bother to train during the voyage. But gold medalist sprinter Ralph Gray refuted that story. "I can certainly remember running laps and doing calisthenics with Jim every day on ship," Gray later said. The two proud athletes challenged each other to sprint races over the deck, which was covered with cork to muffle the sound. Their competition grew so heated that Gray worried they were wearing themselves out. Avery Brundage, no friend of Thorpe's in later years, confirmed that Jim trained as hard as anyone aboard the ship.

Veteran Olympic observers, impressed by Thorpe's all-around skill, predicted the young man might possibly win a third-place bronze medal in the decathlon or pentathlon. The gold medal seemed out of the question, even for a man with Thorpe's raw talent. Norway's Ferdinand Bie and Sweden's Hugo Wieslander were both seasoned international athletes. Thorpe, on the other hand, had never competed in a decathlon. Both the decathlon and pentathlon included an event, the javelin throw, that Thorpe had tried for the first time only two months before.

The pentathlon took place on July 7. The competition included the long jump, javelin throw, 200-meter dash, discus throw, and 1,500-meter run all in the same day. Scoring was simple. First place was worth one point, second place two, third place three, and so on. Whoever had the lowest score at the end of the day won.

The pentathlon led off with one of Thorpe's strongest skills, the long jump. Thorpe soared to a distance of 23 feet, 2¼ inches, easily outdistancing all other competitors. The contestants moved on to the javelin. Under the unique pentathlon scoring system, a single poor performance could bury an athlete under so many points that he could not get a medal even with great efforts in the other four events. Despite almost no time to work on his technique, Thorpe hurled the javelin 153 feet, good for third place.

In the 200-meter dash, Thorpe raced to victory in 22.9 seconds. Bie could manage no better than sixth. Thorpe then stretched out to a comfortable lead in the competition with a first-place toss of 117 feet, 3 inches in the discus.

That left only the 1,500-meter run. Bie could still grab the gold medal if he ran well and if Thorpe lagged far back in the pack. Thorpe could easily falter; distance running was the one area of track and field that he had avoided at Carlisle. Bie took off quickly and opened up a large lead over Thorpe. But the American

Thorpe (second from left) gets off to a slow start in this 1912 Olympic race.
(Courtesy University of Illinois)

gradually reeled him in. On the third lap, he drew even. Looking as fresh as if the competition had just begun, Thorpe stepped up the pace while Bie fell back in exhaustion. Thorpe outkicked all competitors to win the race in 4:44.8. Four first places and a third place gave Thorpe 7 points in the competition, far ahead of Bie's second-place 24 points.

The strenuous effort took some of the spring out of Thorpe's legs. He fell short of his best efforts while competing in the individual high jump and long jump events in the next few days. Yet his 6-foot, 1½-inch high jump was good for fifth place, and he placed seventh with a 22-foot, 7½-inch long jump.

Now the question was, did he have anything left for the most exhausting test of all, the decathlon?

As 29 competitors met on the track on July 13 for the start of the three-day competition, rain poured down on the stadium. Thorpe, who hated running in rain and mud, got off to a slow start in two of his stronger events. First, he slogged to an 11.2 time in the 100-meter dash, good for third place. Then he settled for a disappointing 22 feet, 3¼ inches in the long jump. This mark, nearly a foot short of his pentathlon jump, also ranked third among contestants. The good news was that even those subpar marks topped the decathlon favorite, Sweden's Hugo Weislander. Thorpe completed day one of the decathlon by uncorking a 42-foot, 3½-inch shot put—two inches farther than Weislander's second-place effort.

The clearing skies seemed to recharge Thorpe the next day. He sailed 6 feet, 1¾ inches to win the high jump, then placed third in the 400 meters with a time of 52.2 seconds. Thorpe capped a marvelous day by skimming over the hurdles in a spectacular first-place time of 15.6 seconds.

Having built a formidable lead, Thorpe needed only to hold steady on the final day of the decathlon. He placed third in both the discus and pole vault, and fourth in the javelin. In the last event, when spectators were expecting him to drop from fatigue, Thorpe kept up a relentless pace in the 1,500-meter run. He glided to victory in 4:40.1, more than 4 seconds faster than his winning 1,500 run in the pentathlon.

Unlike the pentathlon, decathlon scoring is based on times and distances achieved, not place. Thorpe amassed 8,413 points in the decathlon, nearly 700 more than silver medalist Weislander. Despite his poor start and the sloppy weather conditions, he set an Olympic mark that stood for 20 years.

Word of Thorpe's triumph reached the United States long before Thorpe did. By the time the Olympic team reached shore, Americans were clamoring for a look at this Indian superman. Thousands lined the sidewalks for a parade in his honor through New York City, screaming his name and littering the streets with confetti.

The near riot overwhelmed Thorpe. "I heard people yelling my name," he said, "and I couldn't realize how one fellow would have so many friends." He pulled his hat down over his eyes and stared at the floor of the automobile as the ticker tape fluttered down on him. When asked to give a speech at a ceremony a few days later, Thorpe did little more than mumble his thanks and then sit down. Many observers, misunderstanding his reaction to the adulation, were miffed at his "arrogance."

Thorpe could easily have turned his fame into fortune.

Promoters offered him $10,000 to make a public appearance tour of the country. But he turned down the opportunity so that he could return to Carlisle for one more season of the sport he loved best—football. The Olympic champion virtually carried the Carlisle team on his back in 1912, as the Indians romped to a 12–1–1 record.

Already a national celebrity, Thorpe rose to legendary status with his play against Army. The fleet running back romped through the entire Army defense for a 92-yard touchdown run only to have the play called back because of a penalty on Carlisle. Undaunted, Thorpe provided an instant replay, racing 97 yards for a touchdown on the very next play.

Even Pennsylvania, the only team to defeat Carlisle, walked off the field with Thorpe's footprints all over their jerseys. Thorpe scored on touchdown runs of 60, 75, and 85 yards in the losing effort. He finished his career by scoring three touchdowns and kicking two field goals against Brown, which gave him an incredible total of 25 touchdowns and 198 points for the season.

That January, an obscure newspaper reporter did what no opponent had been able to do on any playing surface—he dealt Thorpe a humiliating defeat. While interviewing a minor league baseball manager, a reporter for Massachusetts's *Worcester Telegram* studied photographs in the manager's office. There was Jim Thorpe in a photograph of the manager's 1909 team! The next day the reporter broke the story that the world famous athlete may have violated Olympic rules that barred professionals from competing.

Thorpe replied that he played sports for fun and not money, an argument supported by his rejection of the $10,000 touring offer. Furthermore, he had not been aware that he was violating Olympic rules. In a letter to the Amateur Athletic Union (AAU), he wrote, "I was not wise in the ways of the world and did not realize this was wrong, and that it would make me a professional in track sports."

The public strongly backed Thorpe, but neither the AAU nor the International Olympic Committee (IOC) excused his conduct. Olympic officials claimed that the purity of the Olympic Games

Thorpe pounds the football into the sky during a game in October 1912.
(Cumberland County Historical Society)

was at stake. They declared that professional athletes such as Thorpe would tarnish the Olympic ideal of promoting physical excellence among amateur athletes. But under the surface lurked less noble motives. The Olympics were run by aristocrats who wanted to "keep out undesirables," as one historian put it. These people preferred to restrict the games to wealthy, well-bred folks who had money and leisure time to spend on nonpaying amateur sports. They considered anyone who earned money through physical labor a professional. Olympic officials even tried to bar American rower John Kelly from the 1924 games on the grounds that he was a bricklayer.

The AAU and IOC scratched Thorpe's name from the record books and stripped him of his Olympic medals. Thorpe kept quiet about the controversy and acted as though the loss of his medals did not disturb him. But John Meyers, who roomed with Thorpe the next year, remembered one late night when Jim entered the room in tears. "The king of Sweden gave me those trophies," Thorpe sobbed. "I won them fair and square."

"It broke his heart and he never really recovered," Meyers concluded.

Since he was officially known as a professional, Thorpe decided he might as well earn his living from sports. At that time, baseball was the only pro sport that paid a decent salary. In the spring of 1913, Thorpe signed a contract with the New York Giants baseball club for about $6,000 per year. It was an unfortunate decision. Even counting his summer league adventures, Thorpe had played relatively little baseball. He needed a season or two in the minor leagues to learn the game and develop his talent. But the Giants kept him on their major league team, eager to use his fame to attract paying customers.

Worse yet, Thorpe's personality and values clashed with those of New York's combative manager John McGraw. A little man with a huge ego, McGraw said one summer that his team had a chance to win the pennant "if my brains hold out." Baseball meant everything to him, and he sometimes crossed the bounds of fair play to win. He was well-known for tripping and blocking base runners while the umpire watched the flight of the ball to the outfield.

John Meyers, a dedicated baseball man who stayed on McGraw's good side, learned to respect and admire his manager. But McGraw could not hope to understand a man with Thorpe's easygoing nature who divided his interest between a variety of sports. McGraw dismissed him as lazy and claimed that Thorpe could not hit a curve ball. Despite his raw talent, Thorpe spent more time on the bench than on the field for the Giants.

Thorpe never concentrated on developing his baseball skills. When the 1913 season ended, he signed on with Indiana University as an assistant football coach. Soon he put most of his effort into that sport. After six disappointing seasons with New York, Thorpe was released by the Giants. Freed from McGraw's control, Thorpe did show signs of brilliance. He batted .327 for Boston in 1919. Playing in the top-level minor league, he batted .365 for Akron in 1920 and .358 for Toledo in 1921.

But that was for his own amusement and to earn cash. Football remained his first love. The problem was in finding an outlet for his skills. In the early 20th century, football was strictly a college game. Pro football existed only as a novelty in scattered areas of the Midwest, particularly western Ohio. Looking for a way to attract fans, those Ohio teams jumped at the chance to sign the world-famous Olympic hero and college football hero.

Thorpe, more than any other player, brought respect to pro football. Unlike many mercenary college athletes who played one game for a team and then jumped to another team the next game for better pay, he made a firm commitment to the Canton Bulldogs.

As a player, he could beat opponents just about any way he chose. In the open field, he could fake tacklers off their feet or jet past them with a burst of Olympic speed. "As a halfback he is probably seen best whirling, twisting, dancing, and plunging, bewildering his opponents with little pantherlike leaps," according to one newspaper account. When hemmed in, Thorpe hurled his nearly 200 pounds of muscle into the pile to see how far he could move it.

Thorpe's zest for violent collisions proved dangerous to opponents. In a 1915 contest against the Massillon Tigers, he could not get untracked early in the game. Massillon's Knute Rockne (later a legendary coach at Notre Dame) twice tripped up Thorpe behind the line of scrimmage.

Thorpe, on his next carry, roared straight for Rockne. Thorpe's knee smashed into Rockne's head. The tackler keeled over, stunned, while Thorpe kept going. On his way back to the huddle, Thorpe tapped Rockne on the shoulder. "That's better, Knute. These people want to see Big Jim run."

Thorpe was right about his value to the fledgling pro football league. Many of the fans, reporters, and photographers who flocked to the Canton games came to see Thorpe. Jim occasionally put on a show for them before the game as well. Once he awed a pregame crowd by punting a football 100 yards on the fly. That widely witnessed exhibition lent support to unverified reports that Thorpe kicked a 90-yard punt and a 75-yard field goal while playing for Canton.

Sloppy record keeping was just one example of the chaotic state of pro football in 1919. The league needed to get organized if it hoped to earn respect and loyalty from fans. League officials knew that Thorpe was the one star who could give their efforts instant respect. In the fall of 1920, they named Thorpe president of the new American Professional Football Association. Jim served only one year in this ceremonial post. But that was enough to get the new league, which soon changed its name to the National Football League, established.

While operating in the white sports world, Thorpe maintained his ties to his Indian heritage. He took an active part in tribal affairs in Oklahoma. For a brief time, he brought Indians onto center stage in pro football. That occurred in 1922 when one of his hunting partners, Walter Lingo, was looking for a way to promote his dog-breeding operation, the Oorang Airedale Kennels. He and Thorpe hatched a plan to field an all-Indian pro football team sponsored by Lingo's kennels. Thorpe served as the team's coach and star running back and recruited ex-Carlisle players to join him.

For a time, the Oorang Indians drew curious crowds. The team performed traditional songs and dances before their games, and Lingo's airedales treated fans to some stunts. But Carlisle had shut down, and Indians were no longer playing college football. Relying on a dwindling pool of older players, the team struggled on the field. The Oorang Indians posted a 4–7 record in 1922. After falling to 1–10 the next season, the team folded.

Thorpe continued to play football for various teams in Cleveland, New York, Chicago, Rock Island (Illinois), and Toledo. By the end of his career, he seldom carried the ball but continued to boom his trademark kicks. In 1928, 41-year-old Jim Thorpe finally called it quits.

Teammates enjoyed Thorpe as a boisterous but generous, fun-loving soul. So did his hunting buddies back in Oklahoma, with whom he spent many of his winters. But Thorpe's private world turned increasingly to loneliness, confusion, and depression. In 1917 Jim's three-year-old son had died of polio. Some say the loss devastated Thorpe even more than the Olympic fiasco. Thorpe reacted in much the same way he had to his brother Charlie's death—he withdrew, disappearing for days and even weeks without warning.

When he was home, with time on his hands, the tragedies of his life bore heavily on him. He was often moody, and he began drinking too heavily. These characteristics made him difficult to live with; his first two wives both divorced him.

After his retirement from sports, Thorpe lost the footing he had struggled to maintain in steering a path through both Indian and white cultures. No longer paid to perform, he had to seek a new living just as the country fell into the Great Depression. Over the last two decades of his life, he scratched out a bare subsistance. For a brief time, he parlayed his fame into paid lectures, public appearances, and bit parts as an Indian in Hollywood westerns. He also tried to salvage his pride by fighting for the return of his Olympic medals.

But Thorpe was not skilled in the white men's ways of self-promotion and sales. Despite nearly unanimous public support, he got nowhere with the Olympic officials or with any kind of career. Eventually he faded from the public view. Fighting illness and alcoholism, he took on short-term, hard labor jobs in construction and as a bouncer for a bar.

In 1950 Americans rediscovered Jim Thorpe. The Associated Press asked nearly 400 sportswriters and broadcasters to choose the best athlete of the past half century. Memories of Thorpe's towering punts, graceful touchdown runs, and brilliant track and field effort in Stockholm flooded back. Thorpe easily won the award with 875 points compared to baseball slugger Babe Ruth's 539.

Shortly after this moment in the sun, Thorpe entered a hospital for treatment of cancer of the lip. He had no money and so was admitted as a charity case. Three years later, on March 28, 1953, 64-year-old Jim Thorpe died at his home in a trailer park in Lomita, California.

His third wife, Patricia, then saw a television documentary about the struggling community of Mauch Chunk, Pennsylvania, not far from the defunct Carlisle school. She made a unique deal with the townsfolk. Jim was buried at the town, giving the area a tourism boost. In exchange, residents changed the name of their town to Jim Thorpe. Thorpe's name also lives on in the Jim Thorpe Memorial Trophy that has been presented each year since 1955 to the NFL's Most Valuable Player.

The honor that would have meant far more to Thorpe finally returned to him 30 years after his death. In 1983 the International Olympic Committee overturned Thorpe's disqualification in the 1912 games and put his name back in the record books.

ALLIE REYNOLDS

◆ ◆ ◆

The Yankees' Autumn Ace

Allie Reynolds, of mixed Creek, Irish, and English descent, re-vived the spirit of Charley Bender. Like Connie Mack's ace, Reyn-olds posted impressive but unspectacular regular season marks and saved his best for when the stakes were highest. With Reyn-olds taking command on the mound, the Yankees were unbeat-able in the World Series in the late 1940s and early 1950s.

While their results were similar, though, Reynolds bore little resemblance to Charley Bender in either appearance or personal-ity. The tall, lanky Bender presented a picture of fluid grace; ex-football player Reynolds intimidated batters with his powerful 200-pound frame. Kind-hearted Charlie Bender conducted him-self with quiet dignity. Tough, combative Allie Reynolds snarled, blustered, and challenged both friend and foe alike when they got in his way.

New York Yankee manager Casey Stengel caught the Allie Reynolds image best when he tried to persuade his top starting pitcher to switch to relief in 1950. "Why, Allie, they see you walk in from the bull pen and half of them faint right then and there."

◆ ◆ ◆

Albert Pierce Reynolds was born in Bethany, Oklahoma, to David and Mary Reynolds on February 10, 1915. David Reynolds, a member of the Creek tribe, was a preacher in the Church of the Nazarene. He would have liked his three sons to follow in his calling. Allie, however, was far more interested in sports. Although smaller than most boys his age, he took advantage of his blazing speed to become an outstanding athlete at Capital Hill High School in Oklahoma City.

After completing high school in 1934, he accepted a track scholarship from Oklahoma A & M (now Oklahoma State University). His track coach wanted him to concentrate on the short sprints. However, not satisfied with his scrawny physique, Reynolds worked on building up his body. He worked himself up from 140 pounds to nearly 200. Then he looked for ways to use that muscle. He threw the javelin and the discus for the track team and, to his coach's disappointment, went out for football.

Fast, strong, and agile, Reynolds quickly worked himself into the starting lineup. "I liked football best of all," he remembered. "Except for spring practice." Eager to avoid those tedious practices, he turned not to track but to baseball as his spring sport. By this time the Oklahoma A & M coaches were waging a tug-of-war for Reynolds's services; even the basketball coach tried to coax Reynolds onto his team.

A three-year starter in football, Reynolds attracted the interest of the Cleveland Rams, who drafted him following his senior year. Although he preferred football to baseball, Reynolds gave in to hard-nosed practicality. He was a family man now, having married Dale Earlene Jones in 1935. His first concern was earning a living. "I thought baseball . . . better adapted to longtime earning possibilities when a guy got out of college," he later explained.

In 1939 Reynolds signed a minor league contract with Springfield, Ohio, of the Cleveland Indians' organization. He displayed a powerful throwing arm, striking out 140 batters in 155 innings at Springfield. But mediocre control and little knowledge of pitching strategy held his record to 11 wins and 8 losses.

He performed well enough to advance one small rung up the minor league ladder—to Cedar Rapids, Iowa, a class B team. There his career slammed into what appeared to be a dead end. He languished in Cedar Rapids for two seasons, posting a 12–7 record in 1940, and a disappointing 10–10 the following year. As one of the few college men in baseball, Reynolds was older than most of the young prospects trying to make a name for themselves. Approaching 26 years of age and stuck in the low minors, he seemed to have made a poor decision in turning down the Rams' football offer.

Reynolds's arm, however, showed just enough promise to win another small advancement, to Wilkes-Barre, Pennsylvania, of the class A Eastern League in 1942. There he finally gained command of his pitches. Reynolds racked up an 18–7 record and led the league in both strikeouts and ERA.

With their roster depleted from ballplayers enlisting in World War II, Cleveland ran short of pitchers late in the 1942 season. They brought Reynolds up to fill out the roster. Called on to pitch only five innings, the 27-year-old Reynolds made the most of his slim, and probably last, opportunity to impress major league managers. He breezed through all five inning without allowing a run. That persuaded the Indians to add him to their roster permanently in 1943.

Reynolds capped a brief Native American resurgence in baseball during the 1930s. When Bender and Meyers hung up their spikes in the late 1910s, no Native American stars had stepped in to replace them. Then came the Johnson brothers, half-Cherokee outfielders from Oklahoma. Roy Johnson broke in with the Detroit Tigers in 1929 by batting .314 and leading the American League with 45 doubles. "Indian Bob" Johnson followed four years later, playing for the Philadelphia A's. The two enjoyed outstanding seasons in 1934: Roy batted .320, while Bob hit .307 and smacked 34 home runs. The brothers finished their careers with identical .296 lifetime averages. Bob's superior power and more consistent fielding made him a seven-time All-Star.

Roy had retired and Bob was winding down his career when Reynolds arrived on the scene with his blistering fastball. Taking over from the absent Cleveland ace Rapid Robert Feller, on duty in the armed services, Reynolds led the American League in strikeouts. The rookie sported a fine 2.99 ERA but, with weak support from the Indians' lineup, lost 12 of 23 decisions.

Reynolds improved to 11–8 in 1944, then reported to the Oklahoma City Air Technical Command to do his part in the war effort. That winter Reynolds suffered a head injury while playing baseball with his unit. The injury was severe enough to disqualify him for further service, which, ironically, left him free to confront line drives whizzing past his head on a baseball mound.

Returning to Cleveland in 1945, Reynolds overpowered American League hitters with his fastball. He relied more on velocity than control, as evidenced by his 130 bases on balls in 247 innings. Such wildness may have worked to his advantage—it would have made batters think more about their safety than getting a hit. Few had much success hitting against Reynolds as he chalked up 18 wins against 12 losses, with a 3.20 ERA.

Bob Feller, touted by some baseball buffs as the hardest throwing pitcher in history, returned to baseball with a vengeance in 1946, striking out 348 batters. There were batters who claimed that Reynolds threw as fast as Bob Feller, but Reynolds got lost in Feller's shadow for most of the season. Reynolds lost 9 of his first 11 decisions. Even a strong finish left him with a disappointing mark of 11 wins, 15 losses.

During the off-season, the New York Yankees sought to acquire a dependable starting pitcher. They dangled popular second baseman Joe Gordon as trade bait. Cleveland, loaded with pitching, offered New York the choice of Red Embree or Allie Reynolds. Like Reynolds, Embree was a capable hurler who had struggled through an inconsistent season. Embree was 29 years old, two years younger than Reynolds and likely to have more pitches left in his arm. But when the Yankee owners consulted star hitter Joe DiMaggio about the deal, Joltin' Joe urged them to take Reynolds. On October 19, 1946, Reynolds got the news that he was now a Yankee. The trade turned out to be the greatest blessing of his career.

To Reynolds, an Oklahoma country boy, New York was a foreign country. He could not get used to the noise, crowds, traffic, or the fast lifestyle. Yankee coach Charlie Dressen sensed Reynolds's discomfort and worried that the pitcher's nerves were affecting his performance. Dressen's solution was to give

Reynolds a shot of brandy just before the big right-hander went out for his warm-ups. The coach plied him with another shot just before the game started and a third after the first two innings.

Reynolds, who was not a drinker, wobbled out to the mound for the third inning. He could barely keep his balance, much less pitch. Furious, Reynolds refused to listen to anything Dressen said for the rest of his career.

Reynolds settled down to business on the mound without any medicinal help. He enjoyed playing for a strong team and showed his appreciation by giving New York fans more than they bargained for. His 19–8 record and 3.20 ERA in 1947 played a decisive role in bringing the Yankees their first pennant in four years.

Reynolds eased into postseason pressure with a 10–3 victory in game two of the World Series against the Brooklyn Dodgers. But with a chance to nail down the title in game six, he faltered. The Dodgers walloped the Yankees, 8–6, to tie the series. It was the last time Allie Reynolds would fail in a crucial World Series contest. Fortunately for Reynolds, the Yankees recovered to win the final game and capture the championship.

Cleveland won the American League pennant in 1948, despite Allie's 16–7 mark for the Yankees. The Yankees responded to defeat by hiring a new manager, a lovable old eccentric named Casey Stengel. Reynolds's combative nature made life a challenge for both Stengel and the Yankees' young catcher, Yogi Berra. As an inexperienced catcher, Berra lacked the confidence to call his own pitches. That was fine with Reynolds, who preferred to take charge anyway. Instead of Berra sending signals to Reynolds, Reynolds tipped off Berra as to what he planned to throw.

Stengel, however, liked to call the shots in crucial situations. Reynolds would not yield command easily. During a close game early in the 1949 season, Philadelphia put runners on second and third against Reynolds with two outs. The pitcher started to give Berra the sign when Stengel called to Berra from the bench. Reynolds yelled at Berra to ignore Stengel. Stengel screamed louder, threatening to fine Berra if he didn't look to the bench for the sign. Reynolds shot back that he would throw a pitch that Berra was not expecting if he listened to Stengel.

Allie Reynolds during his prime with the Yankees. (Courtesy of
Oklahoma State University)

Caught in the cross fire of this battle of wills, Berra was
paralyzed. "Just keep looking at me!" Reynolds growled. Held
by Reynolds's menacing glare, Berra went along with his
pitcher while Stengel raged at him from the bench. Reynolds
delivered the pitch he wanted—a fastball—that retired the

batter and ended the inning.

Reynolds had a nasty streak that neither Berra nor any other player could ignore. Stengel arranged for Yankee catchers to scoop up a small handful of dirt when they thought a starting pitcher was tiring. Like most hard-nosed competitors, Reynolds never wanted to be pulled from a game. When he found out about the signal, he confronted Berra. "I'll fight you in the clubhouse if I ever see you give that sign," he snapped.

Reynolds's meanness expressed itself in his apparent dislike for blacks, who were first allowed in the majors shortly after Reynolds caught on with the Indians. Larry Doby, the American League's first black player, noted that Reynolds fired a pitch at his head every time he came to bat that first year.

Another Reynolds flaw was his lack of stamina, a problem compounded by diabetes. As much as Reynolds hated being pulled out of a game, Stengel allowed him to go the full nine innings only four times in 1949. Yet Reynolds won his usual high percentage of games, posting a 17–6 mark.

New York won the pennant that year and went on to face the Dodgers again in the World Series. They sent Reynolds to the mound to take on Brooklyn's strapping young ace, Don Newcombe. Through eight innings, Newcombe and Reynolds matched each other pitch for pitch in what sportswriter Grantland Rice called "as perfect a masterpiece as one would care to see."

Pumped up by the World Series drama, Reynolds had no trouble with stamina this game. He kept firing through the ninth inning, easily putting down the Dodger lineup. New York's Tommy Henrich finally ended the long afternoon of futility for batters by driving a Newcombe fastball over the fence in the bottom of the ninth. Reynolds, who had allowed but two timid hits, claimed a 1–0 win.

Reynolds continued to throttle the Dodgers with 3⅓ innings of no-hit relief in game four to save New York's 6–4 victory. The victory gave New York a commanding three games to one lead in the series, and the Yankees clinched the title in game five.

That performance convinced Stengel that Reynolds would make an outstanding relief pitcher. Reynolds agreed to make the switch to the bull pen in 1950. However, the Yankees were unable to find a starter to replace Reynolds and had to scrap the plan.

Reynolds continued his World Series wizardry in 1950. He outlasted the Philadelphia Phillies's top pitcher, Robin Roberts, 2–1 in 10 innings in game two of New York's four-game sweep.

Reynolds's spectacular championship efforts cried out for a colorful nickname, the kind that baseball has supplied in abundance over the years. But baseball people have never shown much imagination when it comes to Native Americans. "Chief" has been automatic for Native Americans, with an occasional "Wahoo" and "Indian Bob" passing for variety. Reynolds labored under the same lack of creativity. He was tagged with the usual "Chief" early in his career. After reaching stardom, teammates and sportswriters upgraded him to "Superchief."

In 1951 elbow problems that had bothered Reynolds off and on over the years worsened. Reynolds sat on the sidelines during spring training, unable to throw without pain. One doctor told him that he would need surgery if he wanted to continue pitching. Reynolds sought other opinions. After a battery of X rays, examinations, and consultations, he chose not to go under the knife. He hoped for just enough improvement so that he could pitch through the pain. The Yankees feared they had lost Reynolds for the season, if not longer.

But "almost overnight and as if by magic," according to one news account, the pain eased. After missing all of spring training, Reynolds began to work himself back into shape. In late April, he hurled a few innings of relief. A couple of weeks later he took the mound as a starter for the first time that season, and beat the St. Louis Browns on five hits.

Working as both a starter and reliever, Reynolds pitched better than ever. By this time, he had perfected a sharp-breaking forkball to go with his fastball and had learned pitching tips from teammate Eddie Lopat, whom ballplayers regarded as the wiliest pitcher of his time.

In early July, Manager Stengel selected Allie's moundmate and friend Vic Raschi to play in the All-Star game. Reynolds was left off the team. Allie's first chance to answer the snub came on July 12 against Cleveland. As if Reynolds did not have incentive enough, his pitching opponent was the legendary Bob Feller.

Through six innings, Cleveland never came close to getting a hit off Reynolds. Typically brash, Reynolds scoffed at the long-standing baseball superstition that forbids players to mention that a no-hit game is in progress. Before heading out to the field in the seventh inning, he told Berra to be careful what pitches he called because he did not want to ruin his no-hitter. Reynolds beat the jinx and completed the no-hitter, allowing only two walks.

In the final week of the season, the Yankees were locked in a tight pennant race when Reynolds took the mound against the Boston Red Sox. Reynolds did not have his best control—he walked four batters. But through eight innings, the Red Sox flailed weakly at Reynolds's pitches. Reynolds carried his no-hitter into the ninth inning. He retired the first two batters in the ninth. One out from his second no-hitter of the season, he had to face Boston's star hitter, Ted Williams.

Reynolds bore down and got Williams to loft a lazy foul ball. Although unintended, Berra got back at Reynolds for the abuse early in his career by dropping the ball. Now Reynolds had to beat the best hitter in baseball not once but twice to become the first American League pitcher ever to throw two no-hitters in one year!

Undaunted, Reynolds fired and got Williams to pop up a second time. Acting as if his life depended on it, Berra caught this one. Reynolds's 8–0 victory, his seventh shutout of the year, clinched another title for the Yankees.

The 1951 World Series started poorly for Reynolds as he lost a 5–1 decision in game one. But with the Yankees trailing the New York Giants two games to one and desperately needing a victory, Reynolds got the call. The reliable right-hander came through again with a 6–2 victory. The Yankees then took the next two games to wrap up their third straight title. Reynolds capped his most memorable season by winning the sports writers' award as the United States' Pro Athlete of the Year.

The Yankees leaned more heavily than ever on Reynolds in 1952. Allie responded with the first and only 20-win season of his career and the stingiest ERA in baseball—2.07.

The Brooklyn Dodgers put up a tenacious fight in the World

Series that year. But every time they got within reach of the title that had eluded them for so long, Reynolds slammed the door in their face. With the Yankees trailing two games to one, he tossed a four-hit shutout to square the series. With Brooklyn leading three games to two, Reynolds came out of the bull pen to save a 3–2 victory. With no chance to rest his arm, Reynolds returned the next day and won the deciding game in relief.

The Yankees made it five straight championships in 1953. For the second straight year and third time in four years, New York turned to Allie Reynolds to close out the series. Reynolds won the final game 4–3, completing his streak of either winning or saving all six World Series games in which he relieved.

By that time, his back and elbow were throbbing again. Unable to throw without pain and angry at the way the Yankees had cut his friend Vic Raschi, Reynolds debated retiring. But he returned for one last season in hopes of being part of the Yankees' record-setting six straight championships. In limited action, Reynolds did his part, posting a 13–4 mark. But Cleveland spoiled his final season by running away with the American League pennant.

Reynolds, still ill at ease in the big city, returned to Oklahoma where he enjoyed a successful career in the oil industry. His business success came as no surprise to baseball people. Reynolds had impressed ballplayers with his intelligence and leadership. American League players had voted him as their representative in dealing with management and labor issues from 1951 to 1953. Long after he finished his career, successful oilman Reynolds returned to a leadership position in baseball as president of the AAA minor league American Association.

Reynolds's career statistics fell just shy of the Hall of Fame level. He finished his career with 182 wins against only 107 losses, totals dampened by his late start and early struggles in Cleveland. But his World Series mastery surpassed even that of Charley Bender, and ranks with the best achieved by any pitcher in baseball history.

Johnny Sain, a pitching star with the Milwaukee Braves, paid the most direct tribute to Reynolds's impact as a ballplayer. Asked what he would most like to have going into a big game, he answered, "I'd like 10 of Allie's fastballs."

BILLY MILLS

◆ ◆ ◆

The Final Lap

Billy Mills walked through the doors of the Olympic village shoe store in Tokyo, Japan, eager to take advantage of the store's giveaway promotion. He had heard that the store was offering free shoes to Olympic runners.

Mills, who had made the U.S. Olympic team in the 10,000-meter run, chose a pair and presented them to the clerk. The clerk rang up the total and waited for Mills to pay. "What about the free shoes for Olympic runners?" Mills wanted to know.

No, that was for top runners only. The store manager had never heard of Billy Mills. Mills would have to pay.

Hardly anyone had heard of Billy Mills. During his stay at the Olympic village, not one of the hundreds of reporters on assignment had bothered to ask him a single question.

A few days later, after the shoe store snub, Mills stood on a wet track alongside the celebrities who had been worthy of interviews and free shoes. He was painfully aware of the yawning gap between himself and champions such as world record holder Ron Clarke of Australia. In the next half hour, Mills could easily run the fastest 10,000 meters of his life and still finish nearly a lap behind the front runners.

Yet, incredibly, Mills had just one thought in mind: "If I can stay with these guys, I can outkick them."

◆ ◆ ◆

William Mervin Mills had traveled a long road just to qualify for the Olympics. He was a 7/16 Oglala Sioux born on June 30, 1938, on the Pine Ridge Reservation in South Dakota.

Although they lived on the reservation, Billy's parents rarely spoke their native Lakota language in front of him. Aware that Indian speech was looked down upon by white society, they wanted to spare him any shame that might come from his ever using the language.

Billy's father was a handyman, a person of surprising inner strength. Every so often, he would defeat the carnival strongmen who came to Pine Ridge to challenge proud Indians to matches of strength, and pocket the five dollar reward.

Both of Billy's parents died by the time he was twelve, after which he lived with a sister. But Billy's father left him with some nuggets of wisdom that he never forgot. "There are three things you will need in life," his father had said. "Have a belief in a creator. Educate yourself. And have respect for other people."

Mills also tried hard to fulfill his father's wish that he be an athlete. He trained to be a boxer, which was his dad's first choice. He got pummeled in the ring, but while doing road work to get in shape for his fights discovered that he had a knack for distance running.

Mills attended the Haskell Indian School in Lawrence, Kansas, during his high school days. There he twice won the state mile championship, and in 1956 led his team to the state high school cross-country championship.

Upon graduation, he stayed in Lawrence to attend the University of Kansas on a track scholarship. He continued his rapid rise to the top by posting the fastest mile times of any freshman in the country. He adapted well to life at his first non-Indian school and became good friends with a white and a black student. But Mills quickly discovered that it would not be so easy for an Indian to get along in a white society. His request to room with his two friends was rejected, and the reason was plain to Mills. "The town of Lawrence, Kansas, decided that three men of different colors should not live together," he said.

He found that even well-meaning people constantly showed a lack of respect for his heritage. Coaches and teammates, for example, took to calling him "Chief," a name that he detested.

While bearing the brunt of white indignities, Mills suffered equally at the hands of his nonrunning Indian peers. Most of his friends were out of school, unemployed, and unmotivated. They could not understand why he trained so hard to compete at white men's games, in a world in which Indians were looked down on. They badgered him to skip workouts, to join them in partying late and drinking. When Mills refused, they accused him of rejecting their friendship and choosing the white way of life over Indian ways.

Hurt by rejection on both sides, Mills struggled to maintain his dedication to running. But after hearing, "Go get 'em, Chief!" one too many times during a race, Mills suddenly snapped. During a national meet at Randalls Island, New York, he quit in the middle of the race. Mills was sent home on a plane back to Kansas that night. Mills and his coach were never able to understand each other. Despite being chosen captain of the cross-country team, Mills did not fulfill the promise he had shown earlier in his career.

After finishing at Kansas, Mills joined the marines and was stationed at Camp Pendleton, just north of San Diego, California. Again he displayed leadership ability and was made a platoon leader. For a short time he ran for the Marine Corps team. But, weighed down by the constant demands of training and discouraged by the little reward he had reaped from his efforts, he gave up running in 1962.

Something inside him, however, could not let go. His wife, Pat, recognized this when Billy became increasingly difficult to live with during his months of inactivity. She sensed that he missed the competition and that he was haunted by his failure to achieve his goals. An avid track fan, Pat talked him into attending track meets with her. She hoped that the sound of the starting gun, the applause of the crowds, and the sight of runners racing the clock and each other would revive his interest.

The plan worked. Mills could hardly sit still as he watched others run. But he had to ask himself if it was worth competing

Mills demonstrates his smooth stride while running in this cross-country race at the University of Kansas. (Courtesy of the University of Kansas Archives)

again. He was still an Indian, and American sports were a white man's world. He wondered if he could handle the thoughtless remarks and not let them distract him from his purpose.

He decided to give it a try. This time he set his sights on a specific goal: making the 1964 U.S. Olympic team. Far away from the pressures of the reservation, supported by his wife, Mills trained as he had never trained before. Every day he ran far out into the dry hills and valleys, logging as much as 100 miles a week. He broke up the monotony by picking out distant trees and sprinting to them, each time imagining he was kicking toward the finish line at the Olympic trials. Mills kept a detailed journal of his workouts; occasionally he would write an inspirational message to keep himself focused on his goal.

At the U.S. Olympic trials, Mills tried to keep pace with America's 18-year-old sensation, Gerry Lindgren. Lindgren, who weighed barely 120 pounds, looked frail alongside Mills who, at 5 feet, 10 inches, 160 pounds was rather heavy for a long-distance runner. But Lindgren ran effortlessly, tirelessly, and in the end, Mills could not stay with him. As Lindgren pulled away, Mills fought through his heavy-legged fatigue. He kept his composure to finish the race in second place, which earned him a spot on the Olympic team. Mills also qualified to run for the United States in the 26.2 mile Olympic marathon.

Mills had achieved what he had set out to do. Working out on his own, he had earned the right to race at the Olympics against the top runners in the world, including world record holder Ron Clarke of Australia.

As he prepared for the Olympics, Mills kept thinking about the finish of the 10,000-meter run. Despite his impressive string of victories and world records over the years, Clarke had one weakness. As *Sports Illustrated* noted in its preview of the Olympics, "Clarke is immensely strong but lacks a sprint."

In a race as long as 10,000 meters, Clarke generally could wear down the opposition long before the final lap of the race and therefore could get by without great speed. Yet Clarke's slow finish presented a tempting target. Mills could see that tape stretched across the track at the finish line. Imagining himself rocketing down the final straightaway in front of a packed stadium, Mills blazed a time of 23.6 seconds in a 200-meter run during a workout a few days before the race. While that was not world-class time, he knew that no other 10,000-meter runner could match that speed. Somehow, he hoped he could cling to Clarke through the murderous pace the Australian would set. If he could stay with the leaders until the final half-lap, he was certain he could outsprint Clarke, or anyone else in the field, to that tape.

That, however, was an enormous if. Mills's dream of a big finish was a nice dream but a little out of touch with reality. This was a 10,000-meter run, not a sprint. Only by running the best race of his life, a time of 29 minutes, 10.4 seconds, had Mills managed to even qualify for this Olympic race. That personal best clocking was still nearly a full minute slower than Clarke's world record of 28:15.6. In order to stay with Clarke, Mills would have to run the first 5,000 meters faster than he had ever run that distance in his life. Then, without a second to catch his breath, he would have to run the second 5,000 meters even faster!

Even Gerry Lindgren had only a slim chance of breaking into the medals. Since Hopi Indian Lewis Tewanima took second place way back in 1912, no American had ever won a medal of any kind in the Olympic 10,000 meters. The 1964 field shaped up to be one of the strongest ever. Although Clarke was the favorite, experts predicted that he would have his hands full fending off experienced international racers such as defending Olympic 10,000-meter champion Pyotr Bolotnikov of the Soviet Union and the defending Olympic 5,000-meter gold medalist, Murray Halberg of New Zealand.

On October 14, Mills took his place among the 36 starters on a track that was still wet and soft from a morning rain. The gun sounded and Gerry Lindgren dashed out into the early lead. Mills concentrated on his strategy: to stick like a leech to the lead pack of runners.

Lindgren blazed the first 3,000 meters in 8 minutes, 20 seconds, with a cluster of runners on his heels. This was a dangerously fast start for Mills, who was fighting to maintain contact with the leaders. He had never before run 10,000 meters at anything close to this pace.

The relentless pace played into Ron Clarke's hands. As the strongest runner in the field, he was confident he would feel strong long after all the others had burned themselves out. Even if Halberg and Bolotnikov managed to stay with him, the scorching pace would drain them and take the starch out of their finishing kick.

The roars of 75,000 fans shook the stadium as they cheered on home country favorite Kokichi Tsuburaya, who was among the leaders. The runners breezed past the 5,000-meter mark in 14:04, faster than Mills's best time ever for that distance. Lindgren, bothered by an ankle he had twisted in practice that week, faded out of contention. Grimly, Mills stayed with the dwindling lead pack.

It was time for Clarke to take over the race. He began a strategy of surging every other lap to break the wills of the other runners. With each surge, Clarke shook off a few more runners. Bolotnikov and Halberg faded out of contention. To the crowd's disappointment, Tsuburaya fell back.

Mills appeared to be the next victim. There was no way he could expect to maintain Clarke's brutal pace. Gasping for air, with a large blister burning into his left foot, he finally yielded to the inevitable. He dropped back a few yards, then watched as the leaders began to open a gap on him. Few runners who lose contact with their opponents in the middle of a distance race can rekindle the will to catch up. But Mills fought off fatigue. Blocking the blister from his mind, he charged back to join the leaders. Again and again he fell back a few yards, and each time he reached into a deep reservoir of will to rejoin the leaders.

With 2,000 meters left in the race, only three runners remained with Clarke: Mills, Mamo Wolde of Ethiopia, and Mohamed Gammoudi of Tunisia. If Mills could beat just one of those three he could claim a medal. With that thought in mind, Mills began to run aggressively. Several times he cruised past Clarke's shoulder and took the lead. But he had no chance of shaking the Australian. The instant Mills let up on the pace, Clarke drove past him back into the lead.

With two and a half laps of the 400-meter track left to run, Wolde dropped off the pace. Incredibly, Mills was almost certain to become the first American in over 50 years to win a medal at

10,000 meters. In fact, he had a solid chance to grab the silver. Gammoudi was beatable. Like Mills, he had never broken 29 minutes in 10,000 meters.

As Clarke started the next to last lap, he looked around to see what challengers remained. When he saw only Mills and Gammoudi, he thought the race was his. He had worn down all his major rivals; these last two were running out of their heads. They could not possibly keep the pace much longer.

Ironically, Clarke's glance gave Mills a shot of courage just when he needed it. Mills misread it to mean that the Australian was worried. "I can beat him!" Mills thought. Shaking his hands at his side to loosen his tight muscles, he moved close to Clarke's shoulder.

When the bell rang to signal the final lap, Clarke made his move. As Clarke burst into the first turn, Mills accelerated with him. The track ahead of them was littered with stragglers who were about to be lapped. Some moved out to let the leaders pass, others did not. Clarke later described the scene as "like a dash for a train in a peak hour crowd."

As they rounded the curve, the three leaders closed in on a straggler who refused to step aside. Fearful of being boxed in, Clarke tapped Mills so that the American would not crowd him. But Mills stayed right on Clarke's shoulder. Clarke shoved Mills to gain some room. Mills staggered.

Clarke had not meant to push him so hard, and he turned to apologize. At that moment, Gammoudi put one hand on Mills and one on Clarke and pushed his way through. Mills, already off balance, broke his stride, and stumbled into the third lane.

Clarke dashed after the streaking Gammoudi, leaving Mills five yards behind. That was nearly the last straw for Mills. For a second, he decided to accept his fate and settle for third. But they were less than 300 meters from the end, close to that finishing tape that he had pictured so many times. "If you run harder than you have ever run," Mills said to himself, "you can win."

Mills found that his stumbling was a blessing in disguise. Lane three was packed harder than the mushy first lane. With improved traction, Mills charged after Clarke, who overtook Gammoudi before the final turn. The fans were shrieking, yet Mills could hear "only the throbbing in my heart."

In the turn, Gammoudi took advantage of Clarke's lack of speed. He pulled even with the Australian and passed him coming into the straightaway. But Billy Mills was flying. He took the turn wide and sprinted by Clarke. Focusing on the finish line, he lengthened his stride and rocketed down the track toward the finish. Thirty yards from the finish, Mills breezed past Gammoudi.

He broke the finishing tape. As Mills cruised to a stop, an astounded Japanese official dashed up to him. "Who are you?" the man asked.

Light-headed and giddy with exhaustion, Mills panicked. Of course he could not have won—he wasn't that good a runner! For an instant, Mills thought he had miscounted the laps.

But the fear dissolved as runners congratulated him. Mills had not only won the race but had broken the American record and set a new Olympic mark of 28 minutes, 24.4 seconds. Somehow he had run more than 45 seconds faster than he had ever run that distance before.

"I'm flabbergasted," he said. "I suppose I was the only person who thought I had a chance."

Ron Clarke felt the same way. When asked if he had been worried about Mills in the later stages of the race, Clarke replied, "Worried about him? I never heard of him!"

Mills enjoyed further rewards for his hard work. He finished a respectable fourteenth in the Olympic marathon that year. The following year, he broke Ron Clarke's six-mile world record with a time of 27:11.6.

Back in South Dakota, Oglala Sioux elders gave Mills a gold ring. They dedicated a building in his honor and presented him with a Sioux name that means, "He thinks very good of his country."

Mills tried to use fame to benefit his people. He worked for a time as an assistant administrator in the U.S. Bureau of Indian Affairs before going into real estate. He used his business knowledge to help Indians understand economic issues that

affected them and to set up the Billy Mills Indian Youth Leadership Program.

He was left with only one regret about what many called the
greatest upset in Olympic track and field history—athletes had
not been allowed to take a victory lap. "I would have loved to have
had the American flag in one hand and an eagle feather in the
other," he said.

Twenty years later, he and Pat visited Tokyo for the opening of
Running Brave, a motion picture about his life. At the conclusion
of the ceremonies, Mills asked to go to the National Stadium.
Although a light rain was falling, his hosts obliged. While a small
group of people looked on, Mills took his victory lap.

Rounding the final curve on which he had accelerated into his
final sprint, he stopped and pulled out a small piece of paper. It
was the ticket stub for the seat where his wife had sat at the 1964
Olympics. Mills paused to look at that seat and then trotted on.

As Billy reached the spot where he had passed Gammoudi, Pat
stepped onto the track and began to clap. Billy turned his head
and let the rain wash the tears from his face as he jogged to the
finish line.

"I needed that moment so bad," he said. It solidified for Mills
that golden triumph that meant far more to him than just winning
a medal. "The real win was to be able to compete with myself, with
all my fears," he said. "I competed with myself and I beat myself."

KITTY O'NEIL

◆ ◆ ◆

Silent Triumph

Kitty O'Neil has never heard the cheers and applause that reward most athletes for their efforts. When she was a top high school diver, injuries and illness kept her from the showcase for her sport—the Olympics. She has set some of her world records in remote deserts with only a scattering of spectators on hand.

But even if she had won the Olympics or had thrilled a crowd of 80,000 fans, O'Neil would not have heard the tribute. She has been deaf since infancy, a fact that makes her wide-ranging athletic triumphs all the more remarkable.

◆ ◆ ◆

Kitty was born in Corpus Christi, Texas, in 1948. In her first months, the tiny infant suffered more tragedy than many people endure in a lifetime. Shortly after her birth, her father died in an airplane accident. At about five months of age, both measles and smallpox attacked her at the same time. "My fever was so high, I had to be packed in ice to survive," O'Neil says.

Although Kitty fought off the illnesses, they left a permanent mark. Patsy O'Neil, a full-blooded Cherokee, noticed her daughter's strange lack of response to the activity around her. Eventually she discovered that Kitty had lost her hearing.

Patsy was determined to do whatever she could to help her

daughter live a normal life. She visited a clinic in Los Angeles to learn how to communicate with Kitty. She attended education classes at the University of Texas so that she could teach Kitty and children like her.

As she worked with Kitty at their home in Wichita Falls, Texas, she endured the frustration of trying to teach her daughter to read lips and to speak sounds that she could not hear. The exercises were repetitive and tedious, and progress often seemed unbearably slow. But Patsy kept at it until Kitty learned to communicate well enough to attend a regular public school at the age of eight. Patsy O'Neil went on to teach other deaf children and helped found the Listening Eyes School for the Deaf in Wichita Falls.

Patsy taught her daughter not to feel sorry for herself or to use her disability as an excuse. As a result, "I grew up believing that I could participate fully in life," says Kitty. She even learned how to play the cello! Although she could not hear the music, she enjoyed the feel of the vibrating strings. She could hit the right notes by sensing subtle changes in the frequency level of the vibrations.

Kitty loved thrills and adventure and never let her deafness stand in the way of her daredevil nature. With careless regard for her safety, "I rode my bicycle down the steepest hills as fast as I could," she remembers.

As she grew older, she enjoyed the challenge of athletic competition. As a 12 year old, she joined a swim team and competed in freestyle events. Occasionally while at the pool, she would cast a longing eye over to the diving board. Diving appealed to her thrill-seeking nature, and she longed to give it a try. But that seemed to be one area in which she would have to yield to her disability. Diving requires a high degree of balance, and balance is closely related to hearing. Her coaches discouraged her from trying it.

When the team traveled to Oklahoma for a meet, however, one of the team's divers failed to show up. Kitty offered to fill in. "I hardly knew one dive from another," she admits. Nonetheless, she walked out onto the board and tried to imitate some of the moves she had seen the others do. Incredibly, O'Neil dove well enough to capture first place. As she held the first medal she had ever earned and saw the spectators applaud, she made up her mind to concentrate on diving.

Six months after taking up the sport, O'Neil won the AAU Southwest District Junior Olympic meet. She showed such potential over the next few years that Dr. Sammy Lee, a nationally known diving coach, agreed to coach her. The O'Neils moved to Anaheim, California, to train with Lee.

Kitty kept an exhausting schedule during her high school years. She attended Anaheim High School during the day. She functioned so smoothly that teachers often forgot that she was deaf. Occasionally, they would turn their backs to her while talking, and she would miss important parts of their presentation. But she worked overtime to make up for the missed information and graduated from high school with honors.

Meanwhile, she spent four hours each day in the water. Lee, who normally shouted instructions to his students in the middle of their dives, had to work out a different method of communication. The best method was to send signals to her by firing blanks from a starter's pistol. O'Neil could feel the shock waves sent out from the gun.

Practices were difficult and often painful, especially when O'Neil smacked hard into the water while attempting a new maneuver. Her body became covered with purple bruises. But despite weighing less than 100 pounds, she was a strong girl and fiercely determined to succeed. "I have to work harder than some," she admitted, "but look at the fun I'm having proving they're wrong." Part of that fun included being named "Young Athlete of the Month," by *American Youth Magazine*.

As she grew more experienced, her coach was amazed at how she could "feel" her way through a complex diving sequence after just a few tries, with a minimum of coaching. When O'Neil won the women's 10-meter diving event at the 1964 AAU nationals, Coach Lee thought she was well on her way to winning an Olympic gold medal.

But during qualifying trials, she failed to lock her thumbs properly as she hit the water at the end of a dive. The impact

Kitty O'Neil (Courtesy of Kitty O'Neil)

slammed one arm against her head, and she broke her wrist. Soon after, a bout of spinal meningitis put an end to her diving career.

Not the type to sit around feeling sorry for herself, O'Neil looked for other ways to combine her athletic skill with her love of thrills. High-speed water skiing caught her interest. She took up the sport with her usual zest, and in 1970 set an official women's record speed on water skis—104.85 miles per hour.

Next she moved on to automobile and motorcycle racing, and she could not have cared less that they were considered men's sports at the time. While racing at a cross-country motorcycle event in 1971, she met Duffy Hambleton, a former bank vice president who had quit his job to become a Hollywood stuntman. Their love of thrills and automotive machines brought them close and the two married in 1972.

For a few years, Kitty lived on Hambleton's ranch where she served as homemaker and mother to Duffy's two children. She never stopped trying to improve herself and to beat the challenges imposed by her deafness. Although she could speak with only a minor slurring, she worked to get better. She would touch Duffy's throat as he spoke, then touch her own throat to try and match his vibrations exactly.

O'Neil also showed an increasing interest in Duffy's stunt business. Duffy showed her his special effects shop and taught her many of the tricks of the trade. Before long she had learned enough to get into the business herself. She found that her deafness actually helped her at this profession. It blocked out noises that could distract her and allowed her to concentrate totally on what she was doing.

Unknown to all moviegoers except for those who read the credits at the end, O'Neil provided many special effects for movies and television shows. With no fear of heights, she jumped off high buildings, and once fell more than 100 feet from a cliff. She drove a car into a spectacular rollover, triggered by an explosive device. On one Hollywood set, she dressed in a protective suit smeared with glue and was set on fire. After a few seconds in the roaring flames, she peeled off the suit, drenched with sweat but unscathed.

In 1976 she set out to become the fastest woman on wheels. The world land speed record for women was 308.56 miles per hour, set by Lee Breedlove in 1965. O'Neil found a small, slender three-wheeled rocket that could carry her much faster than that.

Engulfed by flames, O'Neil performs a daring special effects stunt. She emerged from her protective suit moments later, sweaty, but unscathed. (Courtesy of Kitty O'Neil)

Powered by liquid hydrogen peroxide, the *Motivator* had been built to pack a punch of nearly 50,000 horsepower. That was enough to achieve speeds in excess of 600 miles per hour. O'Neil's problem would be trying to control the mechanical monster. The slightest nudge or overcorrection at that speed could be fatal. Even if O'Neil kept the vehicle riding straight, there was the possibility that the lightweight *Motivator* could lift off the ground at high speed.

In September of 1976, O'Neil went for a test drive at El Mirage Dry Lake in California. Even while holding back the power as she gained familiarity with the *Motivator,* she easily topped Breedlove's record speed. Since the run was made in practice, without precise supervision, the record did not count. But the 28-year-old O'Neil headed off for an official attempt at Bonneville Salt Flats in Utah, confident that the mark was in the bag.

O'Neil shot down the nine-mile straightaway at Bonneville, building up speed. But before she reached 300 miles per hour, the vehicle began to rattle. The *Motivator* bounced, and the vehicle started pulling to the side. O'Neil cut short the trial and gripped the steering wheel, fighting to stay on course while the vehicle pulled from side to side. She held the three-wheeled rocket on course until it stopped, and emerged, shaken. "I was fighting for my life out there," she said. The Bonneville track had deteriorated over the years and had become too rough for such high speeds. But rather than being scared out of any further attempt, O'Neil looked for a smoother course. She settled on Alvord Lake in southeastern Oregon. This dry lake bed, that had once served as an emergency landing strip for the air force, was smooth as a tabletop.

There, O'Neil and her team ran into delays caused by government authorities fearful of effects of the *Motivator* on the environment. Although the unique hydrogen peroxide system produced only water and oxygen as waste products, weeks dragged on without permission.

O'Neil waited tensely, fearful that the first snows of winter would fall before they could make their run. But finally in early December, she got the okay.

On December 3, 1976, O'Neil took a short run in the *Motivator* to reacquaint herself with the handling. The following day, she revved the vehicle up to more than 300 miles per hour to test the stability of the *Motivator* over the flat clay surface. Everything seemed fine. On December 5, she roared down the lake at more than 400 miles per hour on two runs, well above the existing world record.

On December 6, O'Neil was ready to annihilate the record. She squeezed into the *Motivator*, said a short prayer, and pushed down on the throttle. The force of the acceleration kicked her backward and then eased as she picked up speed. Within five seconds, she had reached 180 miles per hour. Ten seconds later, she was roaring down the lake nearly twice as fast as any woman had ever driven before. She topped out at more than 600 miles per hour before cutting back on the power. Five miles later, the *Motivator* finally slowed to a stop. O'Neil had shot through the photocell timing beams at an average speed of 514.120 miles per hour over a one-kilometer (.6 mile) stretch. From start to finish, she had had such firm control of the vehicle that it never wandered more than three feet from the center line.

Land speed rules required two runs in opposite directions within two hours of each other, the average of the two runs being the official time. O'Neil roared off again. This run was slightly slower than her first, giving her an average run of 512.70 miles per hour. She had beaten the old mark by more than 200 miles per hour.

While admitting that she enjoyed thrills, O'Neil insisted that the danger and excitement were not what led her to claim the world record. As always, she had been motivated by an inner drive to excel. "I always want to have a goal, some dream that I can try for," she said. The land speed record was just one more success in a lifetime of overcoming challenges.

SONNY SIXKILLER

◆ ◆ ◆

Football Revival in Washington

The football season at the University of Washington opened in the last days of summer in 1970, to a large collective yawn. Mired in a stagnant program, the Huskies were not only inept, they were boring. While muddling to a 1–9 record the previous year, Washington had averaged a lifeless 11 points per game. The team's greatest recognition from the press was for the racial tension that had caused a number of black players to quit the team.

One year later, Washington Huskies football was the hottest ticket in Seattle. Boisterous fans packed the university stadium to cheer on the Huskies. Stores racked up brisk sales in purple and gold Huskies merchandise. The football team was the talk of pop radio stations, bar patrons, and even a subject of a top-selling jukebox recording.

The person most responsible for turning on the Pacific Northwest to college football was a small quarterback with the swashbuckling name of Alex "Sonny" Sixkiller.

Sixkiller's achievements were all the more striking because of the dramatic decline of Native American athletes in the game of football. He has been a solitary Indian voice in the deafening void in football left by the retirement of the peerless Jim Thorpe in the late 1920s.

There have been isolated cases of Indians playing football in

Sonny Sixkiller (Courtesy of University of Washington)

top college and pro ranks since Thorpe. Jack Jacobs, a Creek
Indian, triggered the high-powered offense of the University of
Oklahoma Sooners from 1939–41 and won All-American honors.
After World War II interrupted his career, Jacobs played briefly

as a reserve on the Cleveland Rams in 1945 and the Washington Redskins the following year. He played three seasons with the Green Bay Packers as a punter and reserve quarterback before moving to the Canadian Football League in 1950. Jacobs found the wide open Canadian rules more to his liking. He won the starting quarterback job for the Winnipeg Blue Bombers and led them to the Grey Cup finals in 1950 and 1953.

Ed "Wahoo" McDaniel enjoyed a colorful 10-year pro career as a run-stuffing middle linebacker. Sonny Sixkiller's cousin, Andy Sixkiller, won All-American honorable mention as a defensive back for the Miami Hurricanes in 1964–65. Bothered by an ankle injury and limited by his small size, he did not go on to the pros. But these few exceptions were a far cry from the glory days when the Carlisle Indians ran wild over the strongest gridiron teams in the nation. The irony of Sonny Sixkiller's emergence as a media darling was that the full-blooded Cherokee star was only barely aware that he *was* an Indian.

◆ ◆ ◆

Alex Sixkiller, named after his father, was born in 1951, at Tahleguah, Oklahoma. He was the youngest of four children, and his family's pet name for him, "Sonny," stuck. Although the great-grandson of a Cherokee chief, Sonny had little connection with his heritage. His grandfather was a Baptist minister, and his family never set foot on any reservation except as curious sight-seers. None of his relations could tell him the origins of his unusual last name.

When Sonny was only a year old, the family moved to Ashland, Oregon, a town of about 12,000 near the California border. There his father found a job as a mill hand, and his mother worked as a maid in a college dormitory.

Sonny grew up as a typical middle class American child, oblivious to his Indian background. He never thought of himself as an Indian—he just thought of himself as "a little person." As a result, he totally missed the irony that one of his favorite games was playing cowboys and Indians with the neighbor kids. "It was really strange," Sixkiller marveled later. "I mean, I was a *cowboy* sometimes. You got to switch off. That's how far I was from the real thing."

Sixkiller was a popular boy with remarkable skill as an all-around athlete. Although smaller than other boys and not particularly fast, he was highly coordinated, quick thinking, and possessed a strong, graceful throwing motion. He was voted All-Conference as a guard in basketball and as a pitcher in baseball at Ashland High School. But football was his best sport. After winning recognition as an All-State high school quarterback, Sixkiller hoped for a chance to play major college football. He especially looked forward to playing for the home state schools, the University of Oregon and Oregon State University.

Both schools, however, took one look at his 5-foot, 10-inch, 155-pound stature and decided he was not big enough for college football. So did most other colleges around the country. The University of Washington, a hated rival of the two Oregon schools, was one of the few places willing to take a chance on him. That fact was an indication of just how low the once proud Huskies football program had fallen.

Sixkiller sat on the sidelines as the Huskies suffered through their painful 1–9 season in 1969. In practice he had shown little indication that he could do anything to pull the team out of its misery. When the Huskies reported for spring practice in 1970, Sixkiller was listed as the third-string quarterback.

Washington's number two quarterback, however, gave up on the football team and went out for baseball that spring instead. So when starting quarterback Greg Collins broke his collarbone in the first quarter of the spring game, Sixkiller was thrown into action.

Taking an instant liking to the team's new prostyle, pass-oriented offense, Sixkiller fired 50 passes in the spring game. He completed 24 of them for 389 yards. Washington's coaches were not sure if the 1970 season would be more successful than the last, but they knew it would not be dull with Sixkiller at the controls.

Sixkiller stepped into the huddle for Washington's first game in 1970 and looked around the huddle. Nine of the ten men gathered around him were veteran seniors. Sixkiller, the sopho-more who had not yet played a college game, was supposed to take charge of this group. Hiding his nervousness, Sixkiller un-leashed Washington's new, wide-open offense against favored Michigan State. Repeatedly, Sixkiller launched bombs far down-field against the shell-shocked Spartan defense. He completed 16 of 35 passes for 277 yards and three touchdowns as the formerly hapless Huskies overwhelmed Michigan State, 42–16. Sixkiller had performed so spectacularly in his first college game that he was named national college back of the week.

Sixkiller disdained the short, safe, ball-control type of passes that most coaches prefer. His go-for-broke style put him at risk for interceptions and incompletions that might have discouraged a less confident quarterback. But Sixkiller shrugged off the failures and kept attacking. Even though Oregon State picked off six of his passes in one game, Sixkiller kept flinging the ball far downfield. With 30 completions out of 50 throws for 360 yards, he finally led the Huskies to a 29–20 victory.

Sixkiller's daring play captured the attention of the networks who put Washington on national television against Stanford. Rose Bowl–bound Stanford featured the top quarterback in college football, Jim Plunkett. But even though Sixkiller was battling the flu, he matched Plunkett pass for pass. Battling back from an early deficit, Sixkiller led the Huskies to a touchdown that closed the gap to 21–20. Enjoying their new image as the riverboat gamblers of the West, Washington went for the two-point conversion. Although Stanford defensed the play per-fectly, Sixkiller scrambled around until he found an open receiver. Washington led, 22–21.

Stanford rallied to win the game, 29–22. But Sonny Sixkiller was the talk of the town after the game. Stanford coach John Ralston said, "We've faced some fine quarterbacks this season, but none of them presents as many defensive problems as Sixkiller. He freelances all over the field, and you never know what he's going to do next."

Sixkiller's rapid release burned other Pacific-10 Conference powers. He filled the air with footballs against the University of Southern California, completing 30 of 57 passes for 341 yards. He performed more efficiently against UCLA, with 18 completions in 35 attempts for 277 yards. Three of those strikes went for touchdowns as the Huskies romped to a 61–20 win over the favored Bruins.

Enjoying fine protection from his all-senior offensive line, Sixkiller broke 10 University of Washington passing records in his first season. He finished the season with 186 completions in 362 throws, and led the nation with an average of 18.6 completions a game. Sparked by Sixkiller's 15 touchdown passes, the Huskies *tripled* their scoring average over 1968, and improved their record to 6 wins and 4 losses.

His role in the startling rebirth of Washington Husky football made Sonny Sixkiller a national celebrity and a local legend. "After a few poor seasons, people were ready to jump on the bandwagon," he later recalled. Stores sold out of purple and gold "6-Killer" T-shirts. "Go Sonny" headbands started cropping up all over Washington. Radio stations played a song called "The Ballad of Sonny Sixkiller," that topped the sales charts and found its way onto jukeboxes all over Seattle.

To Sixkiller's surprise, fans and the media zeroed in on his Cherokee background. Throughout his life, people had made so little of his heritage that he never thought of himself as different. Suddenly, he was bombarded with what he called "all that cornball Indian stuff." Sports reports heralded him as "The Chuckin' Cherokee," and talked about how he was making "heap good medicine" for the Huskies. A national magazine article concluded its profile of Sixkiller with, "It is unlikely anyone is ever going to say, 'Lo! the poor Indian' about this Cherokee." Sixkiller heard more colorful commentary than he could stomach about how he was taking opponents scalps and leading massacres. One publication even came up with the ridiculous report that his father had earned the name Sixkiller by killing six bison.

Becoming an overnight sensation would have been difficult enough for a college sophomore to handle—even without the tasteless plays on his Native American background. "I was dumbfounded," Sixkiller recalled. Once when asked about his family's Indian customs, he snapped, "We don't sit around weaving baskets."

But for the most part, he handled the fuss with a quiet, if reluctant grace. Uneasy with individual acclaim, he deflected publicity from himself onto the teammates. At the same time, he began to think more about his identity as an Indian. He turned to sociology as his major field of study, hoping to find out more about the cultural roots from which he had been severed.

In 1970 Seattle's economy was struggling through a depression. Yet interest in Sixkiller and the Huskies had climbed to such a fever pitch that the university sold more season tickets than ever. With his straight black hair streaming out from the back of his helmet, Sonny Sixkiller orchestrated one of the most complex passing offenses in college. On any play, Sixkiller had his choice of three or four receivers; he would choose his target depending on the defensive pass coverage.

Sixkiller knew that Washington would live or die on his passing arm. The team had no running attack worth mentioning. Fortunately, the Huskies had added speedy wide receiver Tom Scott to catch Sixkiller's favorite deep passes.

Sixkiller started off the 1970 season where he had left off. In the most spectacular game of his career, he rallied his team repeatedly against the powerful Purdue Boilermakers. But even after four comeback efforts, Washington trailed 35–31 in the waning minutes of the game. Starting on Washington's 29-yard line, Sixkiller picked apart Purdue's defense. Four passes gained 38 yards. Then, with just over two minutes remaining, Sixkiller rifled a pass 33 yards into the end zone to pull out a 38–35 win. He finished the game with 24 completions in 48 throws for a school record of 387 yards.

Sixkiller bombed Texas Christian University into submission the next week. He heaved touchdown passes of 56 and 48 yards and set up another score with a 51-yard strike to engineer a 44–26 win. He scored at will against the University of Illinois. After leading the Huskies to five touchdowns in 22 minutes, Sixkiller left the game and watched his team breeze to a 52–14 win.

Sixkiller made the cover of *Sports Illustrated*, an honor he would

Sixkiller's quick release impressed rival coaches and stirred up the hometown faithful. (Courtesy of the University of Washington)

just as soon have skipped. "I would rather the team get publicity, not just me," he said.

Seattle exploded with excitement as the Huskies prepared to put their 4–0 mark on the line against Stanford. For the first time in eight years, the students at the University of Washington held a pep rally. A record crowd of nearly 61,000 jammed the stadium to watch the game, hoping to see the Huskies take a giant step toward the Rose Bowl.

Stanford, however, brought the Huskies back to earth. They crushed Washington's running game and unleashed a furious pass rush against Sixkiller. Sonny fell victim to the *Sports Illustrated* jinx that repeatedly felled their featured cover subjects. He completed only 12 of 46 passes and threw 4 interceptions as Washington lost, 17–6.

Sixkiller struggled through the middle of the season as teams ignored Washington's running game and sent waves of defensive players at the quarterback. But he learned to adjust. With his quick delivery, Sixkiller calmly beat an all-out blitz from UCLA, delivering a 50-yard touchdown pass to Tom Scott to seal a 23–12 victory. In the team's final game, he surprised Washington State by running 32 yards around the right end for a touchdown.

Although they did not reach the Rose Bowl, Washington improved its mark to 8–3. Two of those losses were by a total of three points. Sixkiller finished the season with 2,068 yards passes, including 13 touchdowns.

Washington entered the 1972 season ranked number 16 by *Sports Illustrated*. Sixkiller, as popular as ever in Washington, felt confident the Huskies would make it to the Rose Bowl. The team won its opening game even with Sixkiller sidelined with an ankle injury. After a rusty performance in Washington's second victory, Sixkiller showed the old magic when the Huskies traveled to Purdue for a rematch of their thrilling 1971 game. Washington trailed 21–19 late in the game and were backed up on their own 15-yard line. Sixkiller then fired three long passes for 64 yards to set up the game-winning field goal.

Two more victories gave the Huskies a 5–0 mark. But the team's hopes for revenge against Stanford were dashed in the first quarter of their game. Sixkiller collided with Stanford safety Dennis Bragonier and injured his knee. Sixkiller had to leave the game, and with him went Washington's hopes for the Rose Bowl. Without their star quarterback, Washington generated no offense and lost, 24–0.

Sixkiller missed three more games while his knee healed. He returned with a vengeance against UCLA, firing a 72-yard touchdown pass to Tom Scott on Washington's first possession of the game. But he slumped again in the final game. Washington lost to intrastate rival Washington State to drop their record to 8–3.

More disappointment followed for Sixkiller. Although Washington's athletic department had to shield Sixkiller from all the calls asking him for product endorsements, they received few inquiries from pro scouts. The pros admired Sonny's strong arm and smooth, quick release, but they did not like his size. At just under six feet, and less than 190 pounds, with limited ability to escape a pass rush, Sixkiller did not excite the pros. He went unclaimed in the pro draft of 1973, and realized his football days were numbered.

Since then, Sixkiller has kept a surprisingly low profile for a man who has been called "the most idolized player in the northwest." His most famous exploit since then was appearing in a 1974 football film, *The Longest Yard,* with Burt Reynolds.

With his typical modesty, Sixkiller discounts his role in relighting the fire under the Washington football program. "We were playing well and I was having some success," he said. "The main thing is that they now recognize that period of Husky football as something special."

HENRY BOUCHA

◆ ◆ ◆

High School Legend

Winter comes early to northern Minnesota. The frigid blasts dive down from the Arctic before Thanksgiving, locking the rivers and lakes in an ice grip until April. Long ago, children in this part of the country learned that since you can't beat the long winter you may as well join it. Rather than huddle indoors all winter, they strap on their skates and race across the frictionless surface of frozen water.

Henry Boucha did what the neighbor children had been doing for decades. Only he did it better and with more flair than any Minnesota youngster had ever done before. While still in high school, Boucha had an entire state eating out of his hand.

Most American hockey fans cannot imagine anything that could equal the U.S.'s "Miracle on Ice" victory over the vaunted Soviet team in the 1980 Olympics. But Minnesota hockey buffs remember a game just as intense, as thrilling, as impossible—a game in which a nearsighted high school boy transformed an ice rink into a seething cauldron of raw emotion.

◆ ◆ ◆

Henry Boucha was born on June 1, 1951, in Warroad, Minnesota. The town of about 1,700 people lies at the edge of the Lake of the Woods, a 90-by-60-mile expanse of water that spills over both sides of the Minnesota-Canada border. Long ago, rival bands of Sioux and Ojibwa Indians clashed repeatedly along the river that ran by the edge of their domains. The site of so many skirmishes became known as Ka-beck-a-nung, "The Trail of War," now known as Warroad.

Boucha's mother was a descendant of the Ojibwa who fought along the Warroad River. Hers was one of a few families that remained on the Buffalo Point Reservation on the Canadian side of Lake of the Woods. She married George Boucha, a Canadian fisherman.

Only a few Indian families lived in Warroad where the Bouchas settled. Henry's mother could speak her native language, and she tried to teach her children some of the Indian ways. But Henry and his three brothers and two sisters brushed off her attempts. They wanted to be like their friends. For the most part, the Bouchas lived no differently than the white residents of the town.

That meant plenty of fishing and swimming in the summer and skating in the winter. For boys living in Warroad, hockey "was just what you did," explains Henry. Reminders of that fact are plastered all over town, from the crossed hockey sticks on the town's water tower to the hockey stick factory that is the town's third largest employer. Every boy in town knew about the Christian brothers, Bill and Roger, who played key roles in helping the U.S. hockey team to a stunning gold medal victory in the 1960 Olympics.

"Ever since I was able to think for myself, I wanted to play pro hockey," Boucha remembers. He would often skate for several hours on the frozen Warroad River. At every opportunity, he joined the other boys in organized games at the town's unheated indoor ice arena. In the days before the Zamboni machine, the players took turns scraping the ice smooth between periods.

Long before Boucha reached his teens, the town's coaches recognized that their hockey program had struck a gold vein—a player even more spectacular than the Christian brothers. The main problem with Boucha was finding the best way to use his talents. Despite being the best skater in his age group, Henry played goalie for much of his early career. As a 12 year old, he tended goal for the Warroad bantam team that won the Minnesota state championship.

He was still stopping shots in eighth grade when coaches turned him loose from the nets and let him skate. Henry immediately made the high school varsity team.

Warroad High School coach Dick Roberts marveled, "I've never seen a stronger skater on a high school level." Forward would have been the natural position for such a skating wizard. But forwards get winded quickly from the furious skating they do and need frequent rest. Boucha's team needed him on the ice as much as possible, and so Roberts put him on defense. From that position, Boucha could lead rushes up the rink but could also fall back occasionally and grab a few moments rest without leaving the ice.

Boucha played other sports as well. His natural athletic skills reminded old-timers of the stories of Jim Thorpe. Boucha would take a break from a high school baseball game to go across the field and win the 440-yard dash for the track team. The football coaches at Notre Dame University noticed such a resemblance to the great Thorpe's kicking skill that they offered Boucha a place-kicking scholarship.

Boucha's success went beyond raw athletic ability. He was driven to succeed. Coach Roberts remembers, "Henry's family didn't have a lot of money, but he was always one of the neatest kids in school. He took pride in everything." Boucha worked hard on the hockey rink to polish his skills. As he became more famous, he took a terrible pounding from opponents who tried to wear him out and knock him off stride, but he neither backed down nor complained.

Boucha earned All-State honors as a sophomore and junior, but failed to reach the state tournament in either year. In his senior season, 1969, Boucha again was named to the All-State team as he led Warroad to a 16–4 mark going into the regional finals. But again the team struggled to get over that final hump. A strong Eveleth team matched them stride for stride, goal for goal. The teams skated to a 2–2 tie at the end of regulation play, setting the stage for Henry Boucha to rise from a fine hockey player to a legend.

In overtime, Boucha suffered a cut over his eye so serious that it required stitches. He left the ice for five minutes to have the work done, then returned. As the second overtime period wound down to a close, Boucha rushed down the ice. With one second remaining, he fired a shot past the Eveleth goalie to clinch the 3–2 win and a trip to the state tournament.

Boucha's press clippings reached the Twin Cities before the Warroad team arrived. One newspaper described Boucha as having the "same silvery stride as an antelope's lope." Minnesota North Stars' coach Wren Blair commented, "He has a fine backhand shot, better than anybody on the North Stars."

Although Boucha had not made a big deal of his Ojibwa heritage, the press was as intrigued with the Indian angle as with his skill. Boucha's strong Indian facial features made him readily identifiable as an Indian sports star.

The Warroad team further attracted support as the courageous little underdog among the eight tournament teams. Minnesota's state hockey tournament had no class divisions. Warroad, with an enrollment of fewer than 200, had to compete against 2,000-student schools from the Twin Cities' area.

When Boucha and his teammates skated onto the ice for pregame warm-ups, most of the crowd of 15,000 at the Metropolitan Sports Center stood and applauded them. The support did little for Warroad, however, as Minneapolis Southwest sped off to a 2–0 lead.

Warroad regrouped and tied the game at 2–2. In the third period, Boucha took over. He wove through the entire Southwest team to the side of the goal, then dropped a pass that Lyle Kvarnlov rammed into the net. Minutes later, Boucha rifled a backhand shot into the goal for the deciding score in a 4–3 game.

In the semifinals, Warroad battled their rival from the north, Roseau. With Warroad clinging to a 2–1 lead in the third and final period, Boucha streaked down the left side of the rink. Cruising into the attack zone, he drilled a shot on the net. The goalie blocked the shot, but Boucha raced in and flicked the rebound into the net. Warroad held on to a 3–2 win. Despite the heat of the crammed stadium, Boucha stayed on the ice for the entire game.

That set the stage for the finals against heavily favored Edina, a large school from an affluent Minneapolis suburb. The Edina Hornets, 22–1 for the season, were the swiftest skating team to play in the tournament in years. After blanking Mounds View 5–0 in the first round, they had blasted South St. Paul by a score of 7–1. Few gave Warroad a chance against Edina. But the vast majority of the fans that night favored the small town team from the north. They hoped Henry Boucha could end his high school career with one last dramatic finish.

With Edina leading 2–1 in the second period, Boucha streaked down the right side of the rink with the puck. He shot; the goalie deflected the puck into the corner. Boucha charged after the puck with Edina defensemen close on his heels. Boucha won the race to the puck and shoveled a quick pass toward a teammate.

At that instant, an Edina player slammed into him. An elbow knocked Boucha's head into the protective glass above the boards. Boucha fell to the ice in a daze. The blow had broken his eardrum and temporarily upset his sense of balance. The Warroad star had to be helped from the ice and taken to a hospital.

Boucha refused to bear a grudge about the incident. "It was my fault," he later said. "I made a pass and was admiring it instead of watching where I was going." But many of the fans were incensed. They viewed the incident as a cheap shot that had taken the best high school player in Minnesota out of the game and ended Warroad's valiant run at the championship. As the game progressed, the crowd grew louder and more emotional. Thunderous cheers erupted for every Warroad move; a chorus of boos greeted every Edina effort.

The young Warroad team fell behind 4–2. But in the final period, they staged an improbable rally. Shuffling three lines of forwards in and out of the game, they checked the Edina players away from the puck and attacked the goal. In the third period, Warroad tied the score; the crowd erupted in raucous celebration that nearly cracked the foundations of the arena.

Warroad came within an inch of pulling off the upset when a shot clanged off the Edina goalpost in overtime. But Edina ruined the storybook ending by winning 5–4. Emotionally drained fans ended the night with a standing ovation for Henry Boucha when his name was announced as a member of the all-tournament team. The people of Warroad showed their concern by chipping in $1,300 to pay for Boucha's three-day hospital stay.

Minnesota fans hoped to get many more chances to see Boucha play—as a forward for the University of Minnesota hockey team. Boucha strongly considered accepting a scholarship from the school. But at that time, virtually all professional hockey players came up through the Canadian junior league ranks. American universities did not offer the top-notch competition that Boucha needed to hone his skills. Boucha's lifelong dream of playing pro hockey brought him to Winnipeg with his new wife in the fall of 1969 to play in Canada's top junior hockey league. The constant travel demanded by hockey schedules put the marriage under more stress than the young couple could handle. Their marriage ended within a few years.

Boucha took time off from junior league to join the U.S. National team from 1970–72. Although he was not aware of it, Boucha was following in the skate marks of Clarence Abel, a Chippewa from Sault Ste. Marie, Michigan, who had captained the U.S.'s 1924 hockey team.

As the 1972 Olympic Games drew near, the team's preparation grew intense. The team would have to improve greatly to even get a chance to compete in the medal round of the Olympics. Coach Murray Williamson put Boucha on his top forward line along with Craig Sarner and Kevin Ahearn. Boucha also drew key assignments such as directing the power play (when the opponent was shorthanded due to a penalty) and killing penalties (when the United States was shorthanded due to a penalty). Boucha led the team in scoring through the team's grueling exhibition schedule.

Few hockey experts thought much of their chances in the Olympics at Sapporo, Japan. The day before Olympic competition began, the Americans had to beat Switzerland just to earn the right to play with the A group of teams who would vie for the medals.

But Boucha set the tone for the upstart Americans in the opening game against Finland. Fifteen seconds into the game, Boucha scrapped to win a face-off in the Finnish zone. He shoveled a pass to Sarner who fired a shot past the Finnish goalie from 30 feet away. The Finns countered with a goal. But later in the period, Boucha scored to put the Americans ahead. Ahearn capped a marvelous game for the Boucha-Sarner-Ahearn line by adding a goal of his own as the United States won, 4–1.

The Americans then shocked Czechoslovakia by a convincing 5–1 margin before taking a 7–2 drubbing from the powerful Soviets. The U.S. team's earlier victories had put them in position to win a medal with a final-game win over Poland. The Americans took care of business with another outstanding effort. Boucha scored one goal and set up another as the United States romped to a 6–1 victory. The win gave the team second place and the right to stand on the Olympic platform with silver medals around their necks.

Like many U.S. hockey fans, Coach Williamson seemed overwhelmed by the team's success. "We just wanted to be respectable and give U.S. hockey people something to be proud of," he said. "The silver medal was beyond our wildest dreams."

Boucha, however, had set his sights higher from the beginning. "We felt all along we were going to get a medal," he insisted.

Boucha returned home to find himself hot property among professional hockey franchises. With their rosters stocked almost entirely with Canadians, teams located in American cities eagerly sought an American star who could stir up interest among their fans. Boucha weighed two large contract offers, one from the Detroit Red Wings of the established National Hockey League (NHL), the other from the St. Paul entry in the newly organized World Hockey Association (WHA). On February 21, 1972, Boucha disappointed Minnesota fans again by signing with Detroit.

Boucha arrived in the league just as hockey's finest Native American player departed. George Armstrong, the steady anchor of the Toronto Maple Leafs had finally called it quits in 1971 after a 20-year career. The similarities between Boucha and Armstrong were striking. Both were sons of a Canadian Ojibwa mother and a white father. Both stood 6 feet, 1 inch tall and weighed 190 pounds. Both skated at forward and played an active

George Armstrong continues to demonstrate leadership, fielding questions from the press as an executive for the Toronto Maple Leafs. (Bruce Bennett Studios)

role in power plays and penalty killing.

Armstrong made his mark during Toronto's stranglehold on the Stanley Cup in the early 1960s. In 1961–62, he scored 21 goals and assisted on 32 others to help Toronto into the play-offs. In play off action, he added 7 goals and 5 assists, including an assist on the title-clinching goal for Toronto over the Chicago Black Hawks. Armstrong contributed 3 goals and 6 assists in the play-offs as Toronto defended its Stanley Cup title in 1963, and tallied 5 goals and 8 assists in Toronto's third straight title run in 1964. A consistent, durable player, Armstrong played in 1,187 regular games for Toronto, scoring 296 goals and assisting on 417 others, numbers that earned him a spot in the NHL Hall of Fame.

In addition, Armstrong earned a reputation as a leader and a model citizen. The Maple Leafs looked up to him as their captain for several seasons. Armstrong won the first Charlie Conacher Memorial Trophy for his outstanding charitable work.

Henry Boucha immediately showed that he was headed for the same type of career. In his first NHL game, the Red Wings skated listlessly and fell behind, 4–0. Boucha then charged into the attack zone and whipped a shot into the net. That woke up his teammates, who rallied for a 5–4 victory.

Unfortunately, Boucha's wave of success finally washed out on the shore. After the grueling preparation for the Olympics and the thrill of that upset silver medal victory, Boucha found the everyday grind of pro hockey to be a letdown. For the first time in his career, he had trouble keeping up his intensity. The Detroit rookie fell into a scoring slump. The longer he went without scoring, the more frustrated he became. His confidence drained with each game. Things he had been doing naturally for years suddenly seemed awkward. Boucha finished the final 15 games of the season without a goal or even an assist.

Detroit suggested that Boucha go down to the minor leagues to recover his confidence. The rookie swallowed his pride and agreed to start the 1972–73 season at Tidewater of the American Hockey League.

Like many athletes mired in a deep slump, Boucha dabbled in superstition. He changed the tape on his hockey sticks for luck, then went to a new type of stick. When that did not work, he broke a long-standing habit and began playing without a helmet. However, he found that sweat and his fashionably long black hair kept getting into his eyes as he skated. That irritated his contact lenses. Rather than go back to wearing a helmet, Boucha wore a sweatband.

Away from the pro spotlight, Boucha relaxed and fought his way out of his slump. After seven games at Tidewater, he returned to the Red Wings, still a rookie according to league rules. This time the Detroit fans saw the confident, hard-skating forward that had wowed Minnesota crowds. Boucha played all skating positions for Detroit. He was at his best when his team had to play short-handed. Using his speed and aggressiveness to cover the open ice, Boucha ranked second in the league in penalty killing in 1972–73.

On January 28, 1973, Boucha shot his way into the record books with an explosive start against the Montreal Canadiens. He controlled the puck off the opening face-off, raced through the defense, and lifted the puck past the startled goalie. The entire

Wearing his trademark headband, Henry Boucha glides across the blue line for the Detroit Red Wings. (Bruce Bennett Studios)

sequence took six seconds, breaking a 41-year-old NHL record for the fastest goal at the start of a game. Never one to boast, Boucha even made fun of his own moment of immortality. "It would have been four seconds if I didn't flutter my backhand," he said with a laugh.

Boucha's all-around play earned the Red Wings' Rookie of the Year award. But he was surprised to find that his headband attracted more attention than his play. Fans assumed that Boucha wore the headbands, red during road games and white during home games to coordinate with the Red Wings' uniforms, as a part of his Native American identity. For a time, paper headbands with feathers were a hot-selling novelty item among fans. Native American activists denounced Boucha's headband and the sales that went along with it. They criticized Boucha for exploiting his Indian background to make money.

Boucha admitted that the headbands had become a gimmick. "But I don't mind people thinking of me as an Indian," he replied to the critics. "It is part of my heritage and I'm proud of it."

When Boucha joined the NHL in 1971, coaches and scouts had labeled him a "can't miss" prospect. Scotty Bowman, coach of several Stanley Cup champions, said, "Everybody is convinced that Boucha will be a standout in the NHL." Another coach called Boucha a "potential superstar." During his two full seasons with the Red Wings, Boucha started to live up to that promise. After scoring 14 goals and 14 assists in 1972–73, Boucha increased his production to 19 goals and 12 assists in 1973–74.

On August 27, 1974, Minnesota finally landed the native son that fans had been longing to see for so many years. The Minnesota North Stars traded high-scoring Danny Grant for Boucha. Anticipation ran high as the Warroad native returned to the state where he had built his career. Improving with every game, Boucha began scoring goals at a faster clip than ever when tragedy struck.

The previous season, Boucha had taken a pounding from rough opponents. He had restrained himself from the brawling and retaliation that frequently mars pro hockey games. But he had gotten fed up with the cheap shots. Before the start of the 1974–75 season, the normally soft-spoken Boucha had announced, "I'm going to do a lot of fighting this year. I've decided I'm not going to take anything from anybody."

Those words played an eerie prelude to the events of January 4, 1975. On that day, the North Stars were playing the notoriously rowdy Boston Bruins when Boucha ran into Dave Forbes. A young player with limited skill, Forbes was trying to earn his spot on the roster with cockiness and intimidation. Boucha refused to back away. The two dropped the gloves and took swings at each other. The referee banished both to the penalty box for fighting.

When the penalty time had been served, Boucha rushed back onto the ice. He had stood up for himself when challenged, and now it was time to rejoin the game. Forbes, however, skated straight for Boucha and cracked the butt end of his stick into Boucha's face. The blow shattered the right eye socket. When Boucha fell, Forbes continued to bang Boucha's head into the ice.

The attack was so vicious that Minneapolis law enforcement officials hauled Forbes into court. Forbes escaped conviction, but he and the NHL had to settle a suit that Boucha later brought against them.

Boucha tried to come back at the end of the season, but double vision plagued his efforts. He had three major eye surgeries to reconstruct the socket, but nothing corrected the vision problem. At the prime of his career, although blessed with skating and stick-handling skills that were the envy of most of his peers, he simply could not see well enough to do the job. After brief efforts with teams in St. Paul, Kansas City, and Colorado in 1975–77, 26-year-old Henry Boucha gave up hockey.

For a young man who had prepared his whole life for a pro hockey career, the sudden void in his life and the senseless way that it happened was nearly too much to take. He bought a meat company in Washington State, then moved to Detroit to work in advertising. Neither worked out. Boucha ended up living in Idaho, still bitter, doing little but hunting and fishing.

In 1986 Boucha returned to his roots. He moved back to Warroad, where he got involved as a coach in the same hockey program that had nurtured him.

The scar tissue and double vision linger—permanent reminders of a promising career that twice crashed to the ice in a Minneapolis arena. But he has overcome the bitterness. Instead of dwelling on what might have been, Boucha moved on to success in both worlds of his heritage. He has found success in the ultimate white man's enterprise of selling real estate. At the same time, he speaks to Native American groups around the country and works as Indian education coordinator for the Warroad schools. He spends much of his time helping Indian athletes get the opportunity that was so senselessly taken from him.

AL WAQUIE

◆ ◆ ◆

King of the Mountain

Many Native Americans have wrestled with the choice of competing in the white sports world and forsaking their traditional ways, or keeping within their culture and abandoning their competitive talents. Al Waquie has successfully walked the line between those choices. He has achieved success and fame in the white sports world while firmly committed to the path walked by his ancestors.

Waquie, a Pueblo Indian, follows in the long-standing tradition of endurance displayed by the Indians of the American Southwest. As early as the 18th century, a European explorer wrote of these Indians, "Without any seeming toil, they would stretch on, leave us out of sight, and outwind any horse." U.S. army officers marveled at Apache who could go farther and faster on foot than pursuing soldiers on horseback.

In 1891 a Zuni runner completed a 25-mile course "in exactly two hours," according to two separate reports. If the timing was accurate, that feat remains unequaled by distance runners to this day. A few years later, another observer wrote that he had "never known the Zunis to lose a race." Hopi messengers regularly ran over a 100 miles to deliver their news. In 1928 one such runner was reported to have covered 120 miles in 15 hours.

Lewis Tewanima, a Hopi from the Sand Clan near Second

Lewis Tewanima, silver medal winner, in his Carlisle uniform. (Cumberland County Historical Society)

Mesa, Arizona, was one of the few southwestern Indians to demonstrate his ability under the controlled conditions of white society's competition. While attending the Carlisle school from 1907 to 1912, Tewanima displayed stamina that put rivals to shame. On one occasion, he missed the train from Carlisle to Harrisburg, where the team was entered in a meet. Undaunted, Tewanima ran the 18 miles to the meet, arrived in time for the two-mile race, and won the event.

Tewanima used a technique common among Indian runners—instead of running a steady gait, he would vary his pace. His occasional midrace sprints often destroyed his opponents' rhythm. Tewanima capped his career by winning the silver medal at 10,000 meters in the 1912 Olympics, and then returned to his home community to farm.

Waquie's own family was steeped in running tradition. His grandfather, Felipe, carried messages through the mountain passes to Pueblo village communities 20 miles away. His father, Felix, regularly won the ceremonial races that the Pueblo held to celebrate the harvest. Felix was also known for his ability to run down wild horses on the plains. Al's older brother, Robert, won the New Mexico state title in the two-mile run four times. But like most Pueblo runners, Robert turned down scholarship offers and lost interest in running after high school. What made Al unusual among the Pueblo was not so much his gift of running as his willingness to leave the familiarity of the villages to compete in the foreign world of American sports.

◆ ◆ ◆

Al was born in 1951, at Jemez Pueblo, New Mexico, a village of nearly 2,800 people nestled more than a mile above sea level in the forested mountains northwest of Albuquerque. By modern American standards, his people were desperately poor. More than half the adults were unemployed; those who wanted income-producing jobs usually had to leave the village and seek work 50 miles away in Albuquerque. But they were rich in tradition. Isolated in the mountains, they were better able than many Native American people to fend off the encroaching white culture.

Al was the fifth of ten children in a family guided by the ancient traditions. They lived in an adobe home with no modern conveniences. They supported themselves by trapping, hunting, farming, raising livestock, and fashioning most of what they needed by hand. Al's mother, Corina, won prizes with her exquisite pottery and woven baskets.

But while Al grew to know and respect the customs of his people, he learned to follow his own heart. Al was especially fond of his grandfather, who taught him to take pride in being an individual. When Al discovered his gift for running, he faced the same pressures as his peers. He was urged to stop trying to be better than others and to withdraw that talent from the world of the whites. But Al remembered the words of his grandfather, "Wherever there is a big crowd, stay away. Be on your own." Al took that advice and decided to follow his own path.

Al was more than willing to put in the effort to make himself a top distance runner. "I love to work," he once said. "It makes me happy to sweat." Following a successful running career in high school, he broke away from home and traveled to Haskell Indian Junior College. There he twice earned Junior College All-American honors. The University of Kansas, the school that Indian running star Billy Mills had attended, offered him a scholarship.

But this time Waquie drew back. He did not enjoy running on flat courses and around a flat track. He missed running in the mountains of New Mexico, on the sacred paths he had learned from tribal elders when he was young. Even back at home, he had run his best at high elevations. Other runners could sometimes beat him in village races, but when the contest moved into the mountains, Waquie left all others far behind. "When I start uphill, I can't stop," he once said. "The higher I go, the better I feel." Rather than spend two years training on the plains of Kansas, Waquie returned home to concentrate on mountain running.

Al began to live the life of his grandfather. He lived by himself—trapping, hunting, farming, occasionally earning extra money fighting forest fires. For him, running became not a duty but a sacred event, a joyful opportunity to bring himself in harmony with the land that the Pueblo revered.

He would prepare for his mountain runs by singing tribal hunting songs. Then he would dash off along abandoned logging trails into the mountains. He would leave the trails to find the secret paths that led him along the steep walls of the mesas that glowed red in the glare of the setting sun. Up into the high forest country he would run, gaining strength from the land and from the wildlife. "Animals have gotten used to me," he once said. "Sometimes I chase them because their energy can take me a long way." Waquie would run with any wild creature that moved: deer, elk, coyotes, and even bears if he found one that was not hungry. Although deer and elk could bound away from him at first, Waquie could outlast them. Waquie would trail after them until, exhausted, they stopped running.

While many top runners grit their teeth and suffer through their toughest workouts, Waquie had so much fun that he could hardly bear to end the workout. He sometimes stayed in the mountains for several days, living on roots, berries, and spring water, and sleeping out under the stars between runs.

Occasionally, Waquie would lift weights. But other than that, he paid no attention to training methods developed by successful coaches. "I'm just more comfortable in my Indian way," he said.

Waquie developed such strength as a mountain runner that he became known as King of the Mountains among the Pueblo. He relished the challenge of racing the most brutal courses he could find, such as the LaLuz Trail. This was a steep 9-mile trail that wound up to the peak of the Sandia Crest at a 12 percent grade (i.e., the trail rose an average of 12 feet for every 100 feet of trail).

After dominating races near his home, Waquie went looking for greater challenges. An outgoing person despite his solitary habits, he enjoyed traveling and meeting people. As long as he could run uphill, Waquie was eager to compete in the novel offtrack races that were gaining popularity in the country.

When Waquie showed up at the Pike's Peak Marathon in Colorado in the 1980s, he did not exactly strike spectators as a "King of the Mountain." He stood only 5 feet, 3 inches and weighed a lean 112 pounds. His spindly ankles and wrists could hardly hold up socks or a wristwatch. But Waquie's strength was

Al Waquie adjusts a heart-monitoring device he has agreed to wear for the Pike's Peak marathon. (Nancy Hobbs)

exactly where he needed it in mountain racing—in the steel thighs, the large lungs, and a circulatory system so efficient that his resting pulse meandered along at 37 beats per minute, about half the rate of an average person.

The Pike's Peak Marathon was tailor-made for Waqui. He charged up the 8,000-foot climb on the 14-mile trip from Manitou Springs to the 14,110-foot peak of the mountain, then turned and sped back down to the bottom. He not only won the race twice but set a course record that lasted for nearly a decade.

During the 1980s, Waquie traveled to about a half-dozen races per year. The most unusual was the annual race up the Empire State Building in New York City. Climbing 1,575 steps in the building posed a slightly different challenge than running up a mountain trail. Waquie prepared for the race by running up stairs in the tallest building in Albuquerque, the 18-story First National Bank.

Nothing, however, could prepare him for the culture shock of traveling from his peaceful mountain village to the bustle of the gigantic city. On Waquie's first visit to New York in 1983, he stared in wonder at the skyscrapers, unable to speak. "It was hard to believe that this world and my own could exist at the same time," he said.

Waquie overcame his awe to win the race. He returned to defend his title in 1984, 1985, and 1986. The following summer, Waquie suffered a knee injury that nearly forced him to cancel his New York appearance. But on February 12, 1987, he gamely showed up at the starting line.

Waquie burst out to his usual quick start on the lower levels. But on the 23rd floor, the inflamed knee bothered him. Waquie had to slow down and was passed by another runner. At about the halfway point, Waquie fought through the pain and set out to catch the leader. He caught him on the 72nd floor, 14 stories from the finish. Climbing two steps at a time, the King of the Mountain pulled away to an easy victory. The 35-year-old Waquie finished the 86-story climb on a bum knee in just under 12 minutes. "I feel much better now that I've won," Waquie said afterward.

While New York City fascinated him, Waquie found that it was hazardous to his health. The automobile exhaust gave him a headache, the noise rang in his ears for days afterward, and the stale, polluted air left his throat sore for a week. The experience reassured him of the wisdom of his decision to follow his own path in his running career, especially on the days when a twinge of regret gnawed at him for not pursuing an Olympic medal. Back home in the mountains after his trips, he breathed a sigh of relief. "Here I can live like my ancestors, I can be strong and free."

For all of his success in mountain racing, Waquie's finest moment as an endurance runner may have been an unscheduled race against no one but himself and the elements. In December 1991, Waquie was hunting in the mountains with four others when they were surprised by a deadly blizzard. Waquie fought his way through 12 miles of waist-deep snow to get help for his stranded party.

Waquie has tried to be a role model for young Native American runners. Many of these youths are joining him in the ancient running tradition of the Indians of the Southwest. Milfred Tewawina has followed in the footsteps of his great-grandfather, Lewis Tewanima. He recently won the eight-kilometer "Gathering of Nations" run, competing against Native Americans from across the country. A recent coaches' poll rated the Indians of Gallup, New Mexico, as the top high school cross-country team in the nation. If these young Native American runners learn from Waquie how to develop their talents while remaining true to themselves, they could be a major force in world-class distance running.

But while Al Waquie is proud of the honors he has won as part of the running tradition of his people, they are not the lure that draws him to the mountains to run for uncounted hours. Waquie does not run for trophies or even for physical health. "For me it is fun," he says, "but it is also much more than that." Al Waquie runs to refresh his soul, and will keep doing so as long as his legs carry him into the mountains from which he draws his strength.

RYNELDI BECENTI AND SUANNE BIG CROW

◆ ◆ ◆

Basketball Pioneers

Ryneldi Becenti bounced the ball at the free throw line and stared up at the basket. Four seconds remained in the final game of the season. Her Arizona State team trailed the University of Washington by one point. The game was in her hands.

Words of encouragement floated from the stands in two languages—English and Navajo. About half the crowd were Navajo Indians, many of whom had driven five and a half hours along dusty roads just to see Becenti play.

She bent her knees and shot. The ball hit the rim. She shot again. Another miss. Becenti fell to her knees in despair. She remained on the floor, sobbing, until her teammates lifted her and comforted her.

When she left the locker room, Becenti rode with her father and two younger brothers in silence until they found a park with a lighted basketball court. In the still of the night, she began shooting foul shots. Hour after hour, Ryneldi shot while her father watched and her brothers retrieved the ball. Not until 2:00 A.M. did she finally quit.

SuAnne Big Crow faced similar pressure while a high school sophomore at Pine Ridge High School in South Dakota. With the score tied 40–40 in the waning seconds of the South Dakota Class A basketball tournament finals, Big Crow raced downcourt. Although only a sophomore, she took charge. She fired a shot from the free throw line that hit the front rim. In the mad scramble that followed, Big Crow wrestled the ball away from her Milbank opponents and jumped high in the air. As the clock wound down to zero, she launched an arching shot that swished through the net to give Pine Ridge their first state title.

Divided only by the frailest of human fortune, glory and tragedy often swap places without warning. The defeated Becenti has gone on to previously unscaled heights in women's basketball. The triumphant Big Crow had time only to offer a tantalizing display of what might have been, leaving equal measures of grief and inspiration in her wake.

Basketball is intensely important to many Native Americans. This may come as a surprise to sports fans, especially considering the slim roster of Native American athletes who have made a mark in major college and professional basketball. Clyde James, a Modoc Indian, set school and conference scoring records playing for Southwest Missouri State in 1924–25. Jesse "Cab" Renick, a Choctaw from Marietta, Oklahoma, won All-American honors as a forward while leading Oklahoma A & M to a 26–3 record in 1940. He went on to win a gold medal as captain of the U.S. Olympic basketball team in 1948. Renick was so respected that his teammates surrounded him after the playing of the national anthem on the awards stand and carried him off the court on their shoulders.

But these are exceptions. For the most part, basketball has become associated with inner cities, not with arid Indian lands. Native Americans who have competed fiercely among themselves for years made little impact on the national level until recently.

Blazing a path through uncharted territory is never easy, but Ryneldi Becenti has shouldered an added burden in trying to become the first Navajo to win national acclaim at basketball. The howling, packed arenas of major college basketball are lounge decks compared to the pressure that has borne down on her as the great hope of the largest Native American tribe in the United States.

◆ ◆ ◆

Ryneldi was born into the Tabaaha ("Edge of Water") clan on August 11, 1971, at Fort Defiance, Arizona, near the New Mexico border. She was steeped in basketball tradition from the day she was born. Her grandparents had played basketball in the rough, give-and-take Indian style in which fouls were seldom called. Her parents, Ray and Eleanor, met on a basketball court. After their marriage, they had traveled by car to Oklahoma, Colorado, Utah, Idaho, and California to play in Indian tournaments where the prize money was high and the competition fierce. Eleanor even continued playing in tournaments virtually every week during her early months of pregnancy. She once expressed a lighthearted wish that she could have five sons so that they could form their own basketball team.

Eleanor came close. The Becentis had four sons, but the middle child was Ryneldi, called "Sis" by the family. The daughter was the one who developed the strongest interest in basketball. As a small child, she went everywhere with her basketball, dribbling with her left hand as well as right as her parents had suggested.

Ray wedged two poles into the ground 50 feet apart on their land and attached nets so the children could practice shooting baskets. The children used flour to mark the foul lanes and free throw lines on the dirt court. Ryneldi would shoot so long, even in the cold wind that swept the flat, open land, that she practically had to be dragged inside for meals. She played through rain or snow, and in the mud, ignoring the family goats that sometimes milled about her. Later, coaches would have the same trouble getting her to leave the gym so they could go home.

Becenti did not show outstanding natural ability. When she joined the Navajo Nation's basketball league for ages 12 and under, her coach considered her a fairly average player. But her constant practice, and the experience she picked up playing with older brothers soon began to pay off. The Becenti boys allowed her to play with them in pickup games with their friends. Those guarding her started off taking it easy on her, humoring the little sister. But after she burned them for two or three baskets, their attitude changed in a hurry. They started playing all out so that the kid would not embarrass them.

Ryneldi improved so much that she led her team to the AAU national tournament in Baton Rouge, Louisiana. She rose to the level of her competition and played outstanding ball during that tournament, as her team finished a surprising twelfth.

After a while, Ryneldi became just one of the guys. She not only played like her brothers, she looked like them. She rarely wore anything more fancy than baggy shorts, a T-shirt, and a sweat jacket. During an eighth grade tournament, an opposing coach insisted she was a boy and demanded that her team forfeit the game.

Ryneldi grew especially close to her mother, who quietly encouraged her to keep polishing her talents. Eleanor knew she would never see the finished result of that polishing—she was dying of liver disease. But even as she weakened and her vision failed, she would be there in the stands at her daughter's games. During the summer after Ryneldi's freshman year of high school, Eleanor told her daughter, "Don't stop. Play for me. I'll always be there when you need me." A week later, she died.

At first, Ryneldi could not obey her mother's request. Unable to deal with the death, she quit playing for a few weeks. But when she tentatively returned to the hardwood court, she found that her mother was right—when Ryneldi played, she could feel her mother's presence.

As if she needed any more motivation to practice, Ryneldi dedicated her play to her mother. She got up early to fire shots at the rotting plywood backboards by the house before heading to school. When school was out, she spent every free moment playing hoops with her brothers, often well past dark.

Ryneldi moved up to the Window Rock High School varsity as a sophomore. She became the floor leader of the Fighting Scouts, directing the offense with grace and precision. During her junior year, she led her team to the state 3A championship.

The Navajo have such a strong sense of family and community that they often frown on individuals who seek to stand out from their peers. The attention Ryneldi attracted bothered some folks, worried others. After his star player left one game with dizziness and then fell and hit her head on the court in another, her coach feared someone was putting evil spells on her.

But Becenti never let up. As a senior during the 1988–89 season, she averaged 32 points a game for the undefeated Fighting Scouts and was named the Arizona girls high school Player of the Year.

Then came the crucial decision. Many Navajo had played well on the high school level while living among their people. But none had ever gone on to star on the college level. Playing college basketball meant leaving Navajo lands and attending the schools of the whites.

Ray Becenti knew what that would mean for his daughter. He remembered the taunts and insults that had been hurled at him during his basketball-playing days. But distrust of the Anglos was only a small part of the problem. The greater fear of many Navajo parents was that children who left Navajo lands would adopt the ways of the whites and become strangers to their own family. Or the children would get caught in the middle, comfortable with neither the traditional ways of the Navajo nor the modern ways of the outside world.

College recruiters were aware of the chasm that separated Native American high school stars from college success. After being burned by Indian recruits who could not adapt to college, coaches were leery of wasting a scholarship on an Indian, no matter how talented. Becenti, who had focused too much on basketball to get good grades in high school, seemed a particular college risk. But she was able to attract a scholarship from Scottsdale Community College.

Ryneldi was more familiar than those of her father's generation with the ways of the outside world. She had watched and admired basketball players such as Cheryl Miller and John Stockton. She liked popular music and often listened to a Walkman as she practiced her shots. She spoke English almost exclusively, since her parents rarely spoke Navajo in front of the children. Although

Ryneldi Becenti (Courtesy of Arizona State University)

she retained the Navajo's wariness of non-Indians, Becenti got
along well with her new coaches and teammates. Yet the transition
was difficult. Even with the support of her father, who drove up
for every home game, she grew homesick.

At 5 feet, 7 inches, Becenti was tall for a Navajo woman, but she was small for a college basketball player. She had to rely on quickness, strong defense, accurate shooting, and deft ballhandling to get the edge on her opponents. She scored 1,270 points in two seasons, more than any other player in Scottsdale's history, and was named conference Player of the Year and Honorable Mention All-American in her second year.

Her play impressed the coaches at Arizona State University who offered her a scholarship. That set off the astounding caravans from Navajo lands to Tempe, Arizona, home of Arizona State. Several hundred Indians often piled into their old pickup trucks to watch "Sis" Becenti play big-time college basketball. When ASU played at the University of New Mexico, closer to the Navajo reservation, an estimated 500 of the 600 fans were Navajo cheering on the first of their people to play major college basketball.

The Navajo show of strength was a two-edged sword. ASU Coach Maura McHugh recognized that Becenti was "more than just a basketball player to a whole lot of people." She worried that her player "feels such pressure to be the perfect role model, to make every game the perfect game." But while the burden of living up to expectations was enormous, Becenti appreciated the support. She had seen so many young women her age drop out before achieving any success. They had ended up unemployed or with unwanted pregnancies, mired in addiction to drugs or alcohol. She felt the overwhelming pressures to quit school and credited the backing of her family and friends for keeping her on track.

In her first season at Arizona State, the junior guard showed she was a complete basketball player. She played tenacious defense, yet never fouled out of a contest. She stole 10 passes in a single game. She could shoot from anywhere on the court. Becenti startled teammates as well as fans with her flashy, no-look passes. "When she's got the ball, you better pay attention," her coach noted.

On January 25, 1992, Becenti scored 15 points, grabbed 10 rebounds, and dished out 12 assists. That was the only triple double recorded in the Pac-10 Conference that year. Late in the season, she sank 12 of 13 free throws in a one-point win over the University of Southern California and scored 30 points in a victory over the University of Oregon. The highlight of the season came when Arizona State toppled eventual national champion Stanford. Becenti was the leading scorer on a team that won 20 games and an NCAA tournament bid for the first time in nine years. At the same time, she led the conference in steals and assists.

Never one to coast on her success, Becenti kept up her gym rat habits. Becenti hiked to the campus recreation center every night, even after long hours of studying, to shoot baskets. Whenever she felt like letting up, she would think of her mother and go at it with even more determination. After shooting until midnight, she would return to her room and fall asleep with a basketball in her hands.

In her senior year, Becenti set a school record for assists, handing out 17 in a game against Marquette. She was voted to the All-Pac-10 Conference team and went on to play for the U.S. team in the World University Games in 1993.

Opportunities for women basketball players beyond college are few. Becenti set her sights on competing for the United States in a future Olympics and possibly playing professional basketball in Europe. While her father fretted about losing his daughter to the outside world, Ryneldi insisted, "I'll come back home when I have conquered everything."

But even if she never played another basketball game, she has already blazed a trail for Navajo athletes to follow. According to Navajo tribal president Peterson Zah, "She is perhaps the first role model we have ever had. Children listen. We need her to come back here and to be seen physically to explain to them how she did it."

Certainly the Navajo girls were paying attention. During the 1992–93 season, 10 Navajo women played junior college basketball, and one started for the University of Nevada–Las Vegas. Virtually all of the top players at the Navajo high schools of Window Rock and Monument Valley said they intended to go on to college. Many of them had traveled the long road to Tempe and seen Becenti, not only surviving among her non-Navajo teammates, but leading them.

◆ ◆ ◆

In a more perfect world, SuAnne Marie Big Crow would have followed Becenti into the college ranks and perhaps even have surpassed her achievements. SuAnne was born on March 15, 1974, the youngest of three daughters of Leatrice "Chick" Big Crow. She grew up on the Pine Ridge Reservation of the Oglala Lakota tribe, second in size among American Indian groups only to the Navajo.

From the time she learned to walk, SuAnne plunged into activities with enthusiasm. At the age of three, she forced her way onto the tribe's Tiny Tots drill team for girls several years older than she. At four, she sped around on a ten-speed bike. She also served as token basketball opposition for her sister, Pigeon. Pigeon practiced all her offensive moves against little SuAnne, but seldom let her have the ball.

When SuAnne was in kindergarten, a March snowstorm prevented most of Pine Ridge's second through fifth grade team from reaching a tournament. The team's coach asked SuAnne, who happened to be on the court, to play with them just so they could field a complete team. "All I really knew was how to play defense," she said, recounting the incident. "I not only took the ball away from our opponents, but also from my own teammates."

While attending Wolf Creek Elementary School in the early 1980s, SuAnne took some basketball lessons from Pine Ridge's top girls' player, Lolly Steele. "Back then, people didn't think so much about role models," says Steele. "But SuAnne . . . used to tell me I was her role model." Big Crow learned so well that she made the Pine Ridge High School team while in eighth grade. As a ninth grader, Big Crow averaged more than 22 points a game for the Pine Ridge Lady Thorpes, named in honor of Jim Thorpe. She won raves for her tough defensive play, skilled outside shooting, and quick moves to the basket.

The 5-foot, 7-inch Big Crow had an insatiable appetite for sports. She ran cross-country in eighth and ninth grades, qualified for the state meet as an eighth grade jumper and sprinter in track, played softball in the summers, volleyball in the winters, and even played pickup football games with the boys. In high school, she also performed as a cheerleader for a squad that was featured at the Aloha Bowl in Hawaii and the Fiesta Bowl in Arizona.

Big Crow also knew that there was more to life than sports. She set a goal of graduating as the top student in her class and studied hard to keep her A average.

Big Crow achieved statewide fame as a sophomore in 1989 when she went on a scoring binge against Lemmon High School. She connected on 26 of 44 shots and made 15 of 20 free throws to set a South Dakota state high school record of 67 points in a game. Ironically, she credited her defensive work for her offensive explosion. "I mostly stole the ball and went and laid it up," she explained.

Big Crow averaged more than 30 points a game and finished the season with another state record, 763 points in a season. Her final two points were by far the most memorable, as they clinched the state title. Then, despite missing half her junior season because of illness, Big Crow was voted to the All-State team.

Big Crow's value to the team went far beyond the points and rebounds she contributed. She set a good example for her teammates with her hustle on the court and long hours of practice. She found the courage to ignore her friends who wanted her to just hang out with them in the summer and, instead, spent up to four hours a day working on her basketball skills. She kept the team's spirits high with her friendliness and humor.

Perhaps most important of all, she instilled her teammates with her fierce pride in being an Indian. She once named Lakota Fine Arts as her favorite class "because it is part of my culture." A television documentary about problems at Pine Ridge stung her deeply. She called it "very biased" and fumed at how it focused only on the negative aspects of her community.

When the Lady Thorpes traveled to other schools, Big Crow occasionally encountered cruel racism. That "just sent her through the roof," according to her friends, and made her determined to act "twice as Indian."

As a freshman, Big Crow had stood outside the gymnasium at Lead, South Dakota, and heard the taunts and war whoops of the hostile crowd. Her teammates were stunned and hurt. The senior who was supposed to lead the team in their warm up drills did

SuAnne Big Crow   (Courtesy Leatrice Big Crow)

not want to go on the court. Although only a ninth grader, Big Crow offered to go first. As she ran onto the court with the basketball, the hostile whooping grew louder. At center court Big Crow stopped, tossed the ball to a teammate and took off her warm-up jacket. She wrapped it around her shoulders and began the Lakota shawl dance. The gym fell silent except for the sounds of her chanting. Then she took her ball, sprinted around the court and as the crowd applauded wildly, laid the ball in the basket. Bolstered by the courage of their young teammate, the Lady Thorpes won the game easily.

Later in her career, the team returned to their bus after a game and found it vandalized. Someone had painted over the T and p in "Thorpes" so that it read "Hores." While the coaches reported the incident to police, the girls gathered around the bus in shock. Some cried, others fumed, still others slumped to the pavement in dejection. SuAnne sized up the scene and then shouted, "All right, all of you Hores, get on the bus!" The girls broke into laughter and boarded the bus in good spirits. Again, Big Crow had broken the spell of racism by refusing to give in to it. "It pushes me. It makes me want to do better," she said.

Yet even Big Crow worried about her ability to handle a steady stream of prejudice. "I'm afraid about how I'm going to handle [racism] when I get to college and face it every day. It could get to the point where I get violent."

In the middle of her senior year, Big Crow stood on top of the world. She averaged nearly 40 points a game for the basketball team and was voted the school's homecoming queen. Within a few months, she would accomplish the last of her three main goals. She had already claimed the first: a state title. She was sailing along on schedule toward her second: graduating number one in her class. College coaches were fighting over the chance to give her the third: a scholarship to play major college basketball. In addition, she heeded her mother's urgings that she strive to be a role model. Big Crow frequently spoke out against drug and alcohol abuse.

After finishing her career with 2,541 points and earning All-State honors for the third time, Big Crow headed for Huron, South Dakota, for a final high school basketball honor. She had been named a finalist for the title of Miss Basketball in South Dakota and was invited to attend the banquet.

On the morning of February 9, 1992, she drove along Interstate

90 toward Huron, with her mother at her side. Shortly before noon, she fell asleep at the wheel. The car rolled, and SuAnne died when she was thrown from the car.

Big Crow's impact on South Dakota could be measured by the titanic outpouring of support that followed. Coaches and players from around the state sent their tributes, citing her friendliness as even more memorable than her basketball skill. The South Dakota state senate observed a minute of silence in her honor. An overflowing crowd gathered at the Pine Ridge High School gymnasium to pay their last respects at her funeral. In honor of her most memorable basketball moment, the scoreboard read:

Home 42, Visitors 40
Period 4   Time 00:00

After fulfilling her goal of Division I basketball, Big Crow wanted to come back home and work with young people. This, at least, was not denied to her. Under her mother's direction, an old plastics factory has been converted into the SuAnne Big Crow Center, the first youth recreation center on the Pine Ridge Reservation. Through this much-needed building, SuAnne will be influencing children every day for many years to come.

Along with that center, SuAnne left a message and example to inspire people of all ages, especially the young people of the Oglala Lakota, in the words she spoke to an audience of eighth graders, "Many people believe that you must leave the reservation in order to have a better life, but I don't believe that. This is my home. I love it. We just need to work together to make this a more prosperous place. May God bless you and remember we are the future. Work hard and represent our people well."

SELECTED BIBLIOGRAPHY AND FURTHER READING

◆ ◆ ◆

The Vanishing Indian Athlete

Ballard, J. Kevin. "A Salute to Native American Olympians." *Native Peoples,* Summer 1992. This account of the 1992 gathering in honor of the Native Americans who have competed in the Olympics contains interesting current perspectives on Indian sports participation.

Bowman, John, and Joel Zoss. *Diamonds in the Rough: The Untold History of Baseball.* New York: Macmillan, 1989. This history contains a few brief accounts of baseball's treatment of Native Americans and African-Americans, including Bender and Meyers.

Cummings, John. *Runners and Walkers.* Chicago: Regnery Gateway, 1981. This book includes a fascinating chapter on the exploits of famed 19th-century runner Lewis "Deerfoot" Bennett.

Oxendine, Joseph B. *American Indian Sports Heritage.* Champaign, IL: Human Kinetics, 1988. By far the most complete and readable exploration of Native American sports heritage. It includes a detailed examination of the history of Indian athletics, the sociological aspects, outlook for the future, detailed bibliography of sources of further information, and brief profiles of athletes enshrined in the American Indian Athletic Hall of Fame in Lawrence, Kansas.

Shrake, Edwin. "Wahoo! Wahoo!" *Sports Illustrated,* October 26, 1964. This article describes how Indian mystique generated publicity for an otherwise unspectacular football player.

Charlie Bender and John Meyers

Dickey, Glenn. *The History of the World Series Since 1903.* New York: Stein & Day, 1984. Includes interesting accounts of the World Series games in which Bender and Meyers participated.

Ritter, Lawrence. *The Glory of Their Times: The Story of the Early Days of Baseball Told by the Men Who Played It.* New York: MacMillan, 1966. This collection of interviews with old-timers includes an interview with John Meyers, who gives an up-close look at the world of baseball early in this century.

Also see Bowman and Zoss under The Vanishing Indian Athlete.

Jim Thorpe (Wa-Tho-Huck)

Newcombe, Jack. *The Best of the Athletic Boys: The White Man's Impact on Jim Thorpe.* Garden City, NY: Doubleday, 1975. Full-length biography of Thorpe.

O'Brien, Joseph D. "The Greatest Athlete in the World." *American Heritage,* July 1992. Article-length biography.

Wallechensky, David. *The Complete Book of the Olympics.* Boston: Little, Brown, 1991. This large fact book on the Olympics contains anecdotes about Thorpe's 1912 experience.

Wheeler, R. W. *Jim Thorpe: World's Greatest Athlete.* Norman, OK: University of Oklahoma Press, 1979. Along with Newcombe, the most complete full-length biography of Thorpe.

Also see Oxendine under The Vanishing Indian Athlete. Includes lengthy review of Thorpe's career, comparing various biographical accounts.

Allie Reynolds

Current Biography. New York: H. W. Wilson Co., 1952. Capsulized account of Reynold's life and career.

Halberstrom, David. *Summer of '49.* New York: Morrow, 1989. This book follows a season with the champion New York Yankees and includes many incidents involving Reynolds.

Shatzin, Mike, ed. *The Ballplayers.* New York: Morrow, 1990. This encyclopedia contains brief summaries of the careers of hundreds of ballplayers, including Reynolds, the Johnson brothers, Jack Aker, etcetera.

Billy Mills

Clarity, James F. "Billy Mills Finds New Challenge." *New York Times Biographical Service,* August 1981. A retrospective on Mills's accomplishments.

Great Athletes of the 20th Century. Vol. 12. Pasadena, CA: Salem Press, 1992. Includes a chapter on Mills.

Underwood, John. "We Win the 5 & 10." *Sports Illustrated,* October 26, 1964. *Sports Illustrated's* eyewitness account of Mills's victory.

Kitty O'Neil

Bowie, Phil. "The Fastest Woman on Earth." *The Saturday Evening Post,* March 3, 1977. More biographical than "A Rocket Ride to Glory."

Phinizy, C., "A Rocket Ride to Glory and Gloom." *Sports Illustrated,* January 17, 1977. Background information and description of her record run.

Sonny Sixkiller

Blount, Roy, Jr. "The Magic Number Is Sixkiller." *Sports Illustrated,* October 4, 1971. This article on Sixkiller came out when he was at the height of his popularity.

Henry Boucha

Pierce, Charles. "Soul on Ice." *Gentleman's Quarterly,* March 1993. This profile of the hockey-mad town of Warroad takes a long look at Boucha's career.

Also see Oxendine under The Vanishing Indian Athlete. Includes brief biographical information on George Armstrong.

Al Waquie

Diaz, Jaime. "Harmony on High." *Sports Illustrated*, February 15, 1987. Fascinating profile of Waquie and the spiritual aspects of his running.

Shervinton, Sharon. "Vertical Marathon an Elevating Experience." *New York Times*, February 13, 1987. News account of Waquie's most difficult victory in this unusual race.

Also see Ballard under The Vanishing Indian Athlete. Includes some information on Lewis Tewanima.

Ryneldi Becenti and SuAnne Big Crow

Mallon, Bill, and Ian Boch. *Quest for Gold.* New York: Leisure Press, 1984. Contains a brief summary of the gold medal basketball victory of 1948, captained by Jesse Renick.

Rubin, Paul. "Arizona's Shooting Star." *Phoenix New Times,* December 23, 1992. Article focuses on Becenti's basketball career and adjustment to life outside the Navajo lands.

Smith, Gary. "A Woman of the People." *Sports Illustrated*, March 1, 1993. In this biographical profile, the author provides an in-depth understanding of the cultural barriers that stand between traditional Native American groups such as the Navajo and the modern American sports scene.

SuAnne: A Salute of Love. Unpublished compilation of news articles, letters, and statistics about the life and accomplishments of SuAnne Big Crow.

PLACES TO VISIT

◆ ◆ ◆

SuAnne Big Crow Center
 Box 94
 Pine Ridge, South Dakota 57770
 1-605-867-5565

American Indian Athletic Hall of Fame
 Haskell Indian Junior College
 Lawrence, Kansas 66046

Cumberland County Historical Society
 21 North Pitt Street
 P.O. Box 626
 Carlisle, Pennsylvania 17013
 1-717-249-7610

INDEX

Boldface numbers indicate main headings.
Italic numbers indicate illustrations.